'Herr Meier'
Possibilities of cyb

A speculative consideration

Imprint:

Texts: © 2024 'Herr Meier'
Cover: © Bernd Michael Grosch
Responsible
for the content: Bernd Michael Grosch
Ludwig-Zellerstr. 24
83395 Freilassing / Germany

Table of Contents

Introduction: 1
Digital Warfare: Technological Foundations 4
The actors of cyberwar 9
Potential Targets in Cyberwar 14
Strategies and Tactics in Cyber Warfare 19
Ethics and Law in Cyberwar 24
Cyberwar and the Private Sector 34
The Psychology of Cyberwar 39
The Future of Cyberwar 44
"Military Cyberwars and Their Dangers for the Affected Population" 49
Conclusions: 76
Information sources: 79
About this book: 81
The author 82

Introduction:

The term "cyber war" describes the use of digital technologies to resolve conflicts between states or other geopolitical actors. This type of warfare differs from traditional military conflicts because it takes place in virtual space and often aims to impair, disrupt or destroy computer systems. Cyberwar has grown significantly in importance in recent decades as more and more areas of life are dependent on digital technologies. This includes not only military systems, but also critical infrastructure such as power grids, waterworks, financial systems and communications.

A key feature of cyber warfare is its invisibility. Unlike traditional military conflicts, where physical damage and casualties are visible, cyber attacks often operate in secret. It can take days, weeks or even months for an attack to be discovered, and it is often difficult to identify the attacker with certainty. This invisibility makes cyber warfare particularly dangerous, as it can take place anytime and anywhere without it being immediately obvious.

Historically, attempts to use computers and networks as a means of warfare began decades ago. In the 1980s, both the United States and the Soviet Union experimented with using computers for military purposes, but it took until the 2000s for cyberattacks to become a serious tool of warfare. One of the first major incidents was the attack on Estonia in 2007, in which the small Baltic country was subjected to massive cyberattacks that paralyzed large parts of its government and financial systems. This attack is often seen as a turning point in the perception of cyberwar, as it showed how vulnerable modern states are to such threats.

Over the past few years, cyber warfare has continued to grow in complexity and importance. States such as Russia, China, the United States and Iran have built up extensive cyber capabilities that can be used not only for defense but also for offense. Cyberspace has become a new battlefield where nations seek to assert their power and pursue geopolitical goals.

2 'HERR MEIER'

The increasing importance of cyberspace in the geopolitical landscape is closely linked to the increasing digitalization of our society. Technological innovations such as the Internet of Things, artificial intelligence and cloud computing have not only opened up new opportunities, but also created new vulnerabilities. These vulnerabilities can be used by attackers to compromise systems, steal information or destroy entire networks. A crucial aspect of cyber warfare is therefore the constant race between attackers and defenders to close security gaps before they can be exploited.

Another important factor in the context of cyberwar is the asymmetric nature of these conflicts. Unlike traditional military conflicts, where larger and more powerful nations usually have the advantage, in cyberspace even smaller actors can cause significant damage. One example is North Korea, which, despite its comparatively limited economic and **military (with reservations!)** resources, has a highly developed cyberwarfare capability and is capable of causing significant damage to Western targets.

Current cyber conflicts show that cyber wars are already a reality and that they will play an even greater role in the future. Attacks on critical infrastructure, espionage and economic sabotage through cyber operations have the potential to destabilize the geopolitical balance and endanger international security. This does not only involve state-led cyber wars, but also attacks by non-state actors such as terrorist groups, criminal organizations or "hacktivists" who pursue their own political or ideological goals.

Overall, it is clear that cyberwar represents a complex and multifaceted challenge for the international community. The invisible nature of these conflicts, the diversity of actors involved and the increasing dependence on digital technologies make it difficult to effectively combat or even prevent cyberwar. Nevertheless, the ability to wage and defend against cyberwar will be crucial for the survival of nations and the prosperity of their populations in the coming decades.

Digital Warfare: Technological Foundations

The technological foundation of cyber warfare is a network of computers, digital systems and infrastructure that communicate with each other and process information. These networks can be both private and public and include everything from small local networks to global communications systems. Because cyber warfare is fought in the digital world, its success depends on the ability to manipulate, disrupt or destroy these networks.

One of the main technologies used in cyber warfare is the **internet** itself. The internet connects billions of devices worldwide and is the basis for most cyberattacks. These attacks can range from simple phishing attempts, where fraudsters try to steal sensitive information, to highly complex, multi-stage attacks, where hackers infiltrate entire networks to steal information or disrupt systems.

Another important element of technological infrastructure in cyber warfare are **databases and cloud computing systems** . These systems store enormous amounts of information, and a successful attack on them can not only result in data loss but also massive disruption to the organizations affected. Many companies and government entities use cloud services to store and manage their data. While these services typically offer a high level of security, they are still not immune to attacks.

In addition to the Internet and databases, **industrial control systems (ICS) also play** a crucial role in modern cyber warfare. ICS systems control and monitor critical infrastructure such as power grids, water supply systems, transportation networks, and manufacturing facilities. A successful cyberattack on these systems could have devastating effects on civilians, especially if it aims to disrupt vital services.

How cyber attacks work:
Cyber attacks use various techniques to penetrate systems, manipulate or destroy data. The most common techniques include:

• **Phishing:** One of the easiest and most effective ways to gain access to a system is through phishing. This involves using fake emails or websites to trick users into revealing sensitive information such as passwords or credit card details. Phishing attacks are often the first step in a larger cyberattack.

• **Malware:** Malicious software, also known as malware, is a type of software designed to cause damage to computers or networks. Malware can be used to steal sensitive information, destroy computer systems, or block access to important data. Examples of malware include viruses, worms, Trojans, and ransomware.

• **Denial-of-Service (DoS) and Distributed Denial-of-Service (DDoS):** A DoS attack involves overwhelming a computer system with a flood of requests, causing it to crash or become unreachable. DDoS attacks are an advanced version of this concept, where multiple systems are attacked simultaneously. DDoS attacks can bring down large websites or networks and are particularly difficult to defend against because they often originate from a large number of infected computers, known as botnets.

• **Zero-day exploits:** A zero-day exploit is a security vulnerability that has not yet been discovered by the software's developers. Cybercriminals exploit these vulnerabilities before a patch or security update is released. Zero-day exploits are particularly dangerous because there are often no known protections against them.

• **Ransomware:** Ransomware is a form of malware that blocks access to a system or data until a ransom is paid. Ransomware attacks have become increasingly common in recent years and have already caused significant economic damage. Ransomware can paralyze entire companies or organizations by denying access to critical files and systems.

Artificial Intelligence and Machine Learning in Cyber Warfare:

The increasing adoption of **artificial intelligence (AI)** and **machine learning (ML)** in cyber warfare has the potential to fundamentally change the way cyber warfare is fought. AI can be used in various aspects of cyber warfare, both on the offensive and defensive side.

On the offensive side, **AI-driven cyberattacks can** identify specific vulnerabilities in networks and exploit them in a very short time. Machine learning algorithms can be used to learn from previous attacks and develop new attack methods. Such attacks could be able to adapt to different environments and security measures, making them harder to detect and defend against.

On the defensive side, AI could be used **to improve cyber defense systems.** AI-driven systems could be able to detect unusual behavior in network traffic, identify potential threats, and automatically take action to mitigate attacks. AI could also be able to analyze large amounts of data to identify patterns that could indicate an impending attack.

Despite the potential benefits of AI and machine learning in cyber warfare, there are also significant risks. An AI-driven cyberattack system could spiral out of control and cause damage beyond the originally intended target. In addition, attackers could manipulate AI-powered systems to generate false information or undermine defense systems.

Vulnerabilities and security gaps in modern IT infrastructures:

Modern IT infrastructures are vulnerable to a variety of vulnerabilities and security gaps. These vulnerabilities can be exploited by attackers to penetrate systems, steal information or disrupt networks.

One of the biggest challenges in cybersecurity is the **complexity of modern systems.** Companies and government organizations often use a variety of software solutions that communicate with and depend on each other. These systems have often grown over years, and it is difficult to ensure that all components are adequately protected. Vulnerabilities in a single component can lead to attackers gaining access to other, critical systems.

Encryption is one of the most important methods to protect data in IT infrastructures. Encryption technologies make it difficult for attackers to access confidential information even if they penetrate a system. However, encryption is not always secure. New technological developments, such as **quantum computers**, may be able to break modern encryption methods, which would have a significant impact on cybersecurity.

Cyberwarfare in the age of the Internet of Things (IoT):

The **Internet of Things (IoT)** describes the networking of physical devices via the Internet. This includes not only computers and smartphones, but also household appliances, vehicles, medical devices and industrial control systems. The IoT has brought enormous benefits to many areas of life, but it has also created new security risks.

Because IoT devices often do not have the same security measures as traditional computers, they are particularly vulnerable to cyberattacks. For example, an attacker could break into a connected household appliance and use it as an entry point to gain access to the owner's home network. In industrial settings, attacks on IoT devices could result in production lines being disrupted or critical infrastructure being compromised.

Another risk is that **IoT devices** are often deployed in large numbers. This could allow an attacker to compromise a large number of devices at once and connect them to form a **botnet** that can be used for DDoS attacks. Such a botnet could be able to bring down large parts of the internet or target companies or government institutions.

Despite these risks, there are also technologies that have been developed to improve security in the IoT space. These include **authenticated communication protocols** that ensure that only authorized devices communicate with each other, and **firmware updates** that close security gaps in connected devices. However, ensuring security in a world where more and more devices are connected to each other remains an ongoing challenge.

8   'HERR MEIER'

*

The actors of cyberwar

In the world of cyber warfare, there are a variety of actors involved in these digital conflicts. These actors range from state militaries and intelligence agencies to well-organized hacker groups to individuals operating in the digital space with different motives. While some actors are directly guided by state interests, others operate independently or as part of organized groups pursuing ideological, financial or geopolitical goals. This section looks in detail at the main actors in cyber warfare, their motives and methods.

State actors: military, secret services and state-sponsored hacker groups.

One of the most important players in the world of cyber warfare are **state actors**, including the military and intelligence agencies. In many countries, special cyber warfare units have been established within the armed forces to ensure the country's defense in the digital space and to conduct offensive operations against potential adversaries.

Countries such as the United States, Russia, China and Israel have invested significant resources in recent years in building **cyber warfare capabilities**. These cyber units are responsible for both defense against cyber attacks and offensive operations aimed at disrupting enemy infrastructure or stealing sensitive information.

In the US, the **United States Cyber Command (USCYBERCOM) is** the central institution for military cyber warfare. USCYBERCOM was founded in 2009 and coordinates the cyber operations of the American military. Its main tasks include protecting military networks, conducting offensive cyber attacks and assisting other government agencies in defending against cyber threats. The US has publicly stated that it views cyber attacks as a legitimate means of warfare and would respond with appropriate countermeasures in the event of an attack on its critical infrastructure.

Russia is another significant state actor in the field of cyber warfare. **Russian intelligence services and the military** are heavily involved in the digital space and **'allegedly'** regularly conduct cyber operations targeting Western states and institutions. A prominent example is the allegation that Russian hackers attempted to influence the election through cyberattacks and disinformation campaigns during the 2016 US presidential election . Russia allegedly uses cyberattacks in a targeted manner to pursue geopolitical goals and undermine the stability of Western democracies.

China is also said to be a major player in the world of cyber warfare. The Chinese government and **People's Liberation Army** have built up extensive cyber capabilities that can be used for both espionage and sabotage. **Chinese hacker groups** , often linked to the government, are notorious for their (**supposed**) attacks on Western companies and governments to steal technology and intellectual property. These attacks are allegedly aimed at strengthening China's economic and military position.

In addition to the obvious military actors, there are also **state-sponsored hacker groups** that often work on behalf of governments but are not formally part of the military or intelligence services. These groups often operate covertly and can carry out deniable attacks so that the respective state can deny its involvement. This form of "deniability" makes state-sponsored hacker groups a valuable tool in modern cyber warfare.

Non-state actors: hacktivists, cybercriminals and private security companies

In addition to state actors, **non-state actors are playing** an increasingly important role in cyber warfare. These groups can be very diverse, both in terms of their goals and their methods. While some of these groups are financially motivated, others pursue political or ideological goals.

One of the most well-known groups of non-state actors are the so-called **hacktivists** . Hacktivism is a form of activism that relies on hacking computer networks to spread a political or social message. One of the most well-known hacktivist groups is **Anonymous** , a loosely organized group of hackers who advocate for internet freedom, transparency, and against government surveillance. Anonymous is known for its attacks on governments, large corporations, and organizations that are viewed as repressive or corrupt. These attacks range from DDoS attacks to the publication of confidential data.

Another important group of non-state actors in cyberwarfare are **cybercriminals** . While most cybercriminals are primarily financially motivated, their actions can have significant national security implications. Some cybercriminals work directly with or are tolerated by state actors as long as their activities serve the interests of the respective state. For example, some cybercriminals in Russia or North Korea have **(allegedly)** been shown to receive state support to continue their activities. In some cases, states even use **cybercrime** as a form of asymmetric warfare to exert economic pressure on other countries.

Private security companies are playing a growing role in cyber warfare, as they often work as consultants or contractors for government entities. These companies provide cybersecurity services and help governments and businesses defend themselves against cyberattacks. At the same time, some private security companies have their own offensive capabilities and can conduct cyberattacks on behalf of governments. However, there is a fine line between legitimate security services and questionable operations that use private companies as a cover for state-led cyberwarfare.

International organizations and their role in cyber warfare:
International organizations such as the **United Nations (UN)** , the **European Union (EU)** and **NATO** want to play a central role in developing guidelines and rules for dealing with cyber conflicts. While traditional military conflicts are subject to clearly defined rules, such as

those set out in the Geneva Conventions, there are still many gray areas in the field of cyber warfare.

NATO has increased its response to the threat of cyber attacks in recent years, making cyber warfare a key theme in its defense strategy. In 2016, NATO stated that a **cyber attack** on one member state could be viewed as an attack on the entire Alliance, potentially leading to a collective military response. This highlights that, in the eyes of many states, cyber warfare poses a similar threat to conventional military attacks.

The **European Union** has also taken a number of measures to strengthen cybersecurity in its member countries. These include initiatives such as the **Network and Information Security Directive (NIS Directive)** , which aims to harmonise cybersecurity standards across the EU and increase resilience to cyberattacks. The EU also works closely with other international organisations to develop and implement global standards in the field of cybersecurity.

Despite these efforts, significant challenges remain in regulating and enforcing cyber warfare rules at the international level. A key problem is that many states are unwilling to disclose their cyber capabilities or submit them to international controls. In addition, it is often difficult to clearly determine the origin of a cyber attack, making it difficult to impose sanctions or other punitive measures.

Motives of those involved: geopolitical, economic and ideological goals

The various actors in cyber warfare pursue a variety of motives, ranging from geopolitical interests to economic or ideological goals.

For **state actors, geopolitical goals** are usually paramount. States use cyber warfare to secure their power on the international stage, collect intelligence, or weaken the infrastructure of their opponents. One example of this is the increasing use of **cyber espionage** , in which state actors attempt to steal confidential information from foreign governments or companies to gain a strategic advantage.

Economic motives also play an important role in cyber warfare, especially when it comes to **economic espionage** . States such as China and Russia are often **'accused'** of carrying out cyber attacks on Western companies in order to steal valuable intellectual property and advance their own economic development. These types of attacks can have serious consequences for the companies affected, as they can lose their competitiveness in the global market.

For non-state actors, especially **hacktivists , ideological motives** are often paramount. Hacktivists use cyberattacks to draw attention to social, political or environmental problems. Their goal is to raise public awareness or punish certain organizations that they see as unfair or corrupt. These types of cyberattacks are often high-profile and aim to undermine society's trust in certain institutions.

Cybercriminals , on the other hand, are usually **financially motivated** . Their main goal is to make money, whether by stealing data, extorting ransoms, or selling stolen information on the black market. However, cybercriminals can also be supported by state actors, especially in countries where the state is unable or unwilling to crack down on cybercrime as long as it serves the interests of the state.

Conclusion on the actors of cyber wars:

The world of cyber warfare is extremely complex and involves a wide range of actors with different motives and methods. States, non-state actors and international organizations all play an important role in this field, and their actions can have a significant impact on global security and stability. With the increasing reliance on digital technologies and the growing threat of cyber attacks, it is crucial to better understand cyber warfare actors and their objectives in order to develop effective measures to defend against these threats.

*

Potential Targets in Cyberwar

Cyberwar typically targets highly sensitive and critical infrastructures that are central to the smooth functioning of a state, its economy and society as a whole. Such attacks are particularly dangerous because they can not only cause short-term disruptions, but also have long-term and serious effects that go beyond the actual target of the attack. This section examines the main targets in cyberwar and the potential impact that attacks on these structures could have.

Critical infrastructures: energy, water, transport and healthcare

One of the greatest threats posed by cyber warfare is the attack on **critical infrastructures** , which are essential for the functioning of a state. These systems have become increasingly digitized in recent decades, making them vulnerable to cyberattacks. The most important critical infrastructures include the **energy system** , **water supply** , **transportation** and **healthcare.**

A country's **energy system** is one of the most important and vulnerable targets for cyberattacks. Attacks on power grids can have catastrophic consequences, as they can paralyze entire regions and severely affect both civilians and industry. A prominent example of such an attack is the **2015 cyberattack on the Ukrainian power grid** , in which hackers cut off power to hundreds of thousands of people. The attack was seen as a targeted operation to destabilize the country politically and economically. Such attacks can cause not only short-term power outages, but also long-term damage to infrastructure that is difficult to repair.

water supplies are also a potential target of cyberattacks. A successful attack on water treatment plants or distribution systems could leave millions of people without clean drinking water. In extreme cases, attackers could manipulate the chemical processes in water treatment plants and thus contaminate drinking water, posing an immediate threat to public health.

Another critical target is **transportation**, especially at a time when more and more transportation systems are becoming digitalized and connected. Modern traffic control systems, air traffic controller systems, and even autonomous vehicles rely on digital networks to function efficiently. A cyberattack on these systems could have devastating consequences, such as plane crashes, pile-ups, or the shutdown of all public transportation. What is particularly worrying is the fact that many of these systems are outdated and inadequately secured, making them an attractive target for attackers.

The **healthcare sector** is also heavily dependent on digitalization, making it vulnerable to cyberattacks. Attacks on hospitals, medical devices or electronic health records could have devastating consequences. For example, a cyberattack on a hospital could disable vital equipment such as ventilators or heart monitors, which could lead to deaths. In addition, attackers could steal or tamper with sensitive health data, which could shake patients' trust in the healthcare system. A prominent example is the **2017 WannaCry ransomware attack**, which massively affected the British national health system (NHS). Many hospitals had to postpone operations and treatments because they did not have access to their digital systems.

Government institutions and military networks:

Government institutions are another main target of cyber warfare. Attacks on ministries, offices and authorities can paralyze a country's administrative apparatus and lead to political instability. Such an attack could compromise important government data, disrupt internal communications or even shake the population's trust in the government.

A prominent example of such an attack is the **2007 cyberattack on Estonia**, in which several government institutions were paralyzed by DDoS attacks. This resulted in widespread disruption of public services and marked one of the first cases of a country being destabilized on a large scale by cyberattacks. The attack is considered one of the earliest documented cases of cyberwarfare in which state institutions were directly targeted.

In addition to civilian government institutions, **military networks are also** potential targets for cyber warfare. Modern military forces rely heavily on digital communications, satellites and networks to coordinate their operations. An attack on these systems could significantly impact a country's ability to command its armed forces. A targeted cyberattack could disable military satellites, disrupt troop movements or disrupt communications between different army units. An example of such activities is the **Stuxnet attack** on Iran's nuclear program, which used a cyberweapon to tamper with the centrifuges in Iranian nuclear facilities. This attack is considered one of the first known cases of a cyberattack deliberately destroying physical infrastructure.

Another target of cyberattacks are **intelligence agencies** and their communications networks. By stealing classified or secret information, attackers could gain a significant strategic advantage. This could not only endanger a country's national security, but also affect the geopolitical balance.

Financial systems and the economy as a target:

One of the most attractive targets for cyber warfare is a country's **financial systems** and **economy** . Banks, stock exchanges and payment systems are heavily dependent on digital networks, making them an ideal target for cyber attacks. A successful attack on a financial system could cause widespread economic damage and undermine confidence in a country's stability.

One of the most dangerous forms of cyberattacks on financial systems is **the manipulation of bank data** or **transaction systems** . Such an attack could lead to funds being moved from one account to another or account balances being changed. In the worst case, attackers could completely paralyze financial systems, which could lead to panic among the population and an economic collapse.

Another risk is attacks on **stock exchange systems**. A targeted cyber attack on a stock exchange could manipulate trading and cause billions in losses. Even minor disruptions could shake investors' confidence and lead to massive price losses. Since the stock exchanges are globally networked, such attacks could quickly spread to other countries.

In addition, **multinational companies** and **business organizations are** often the target of cyber attacks. These attacks often aim to steal valuable intellectual property, such as technical innovations, trade secrets or customer information. Such attacks can massively affect a company's competitiveness and lead to significant financial losses. Particularly dangerous are attacks on **supply chains** , in which hackers specifically exploit vulnerabilities in suppliers' networks to gain access to the networks of large companies.

Cyberattacks on **financial and economic systems** also have a strong **psychological impact.** The public's trust in the security of the banking system and economic infrastructure can be severely damaged by such attacks. This could lead to bank runs, mass panic and long-term economic damage that goes far beyond the direct impact of the attack.

Media, disinformation and information wars:

In addition to physical attacks on infrastructure, **media** and **information warfare also play** a central role in cyber warfare. Modern conflicts are increasingly being fought at the **information level** , where the aim is to influence public opinion, promote political instability or undermine the credibility of governments.

A central element of this strategy is the spread of **disinformation** . Cyber warriors often use social media and online platforms to spread fake news or manipulative content aimed at dividing the population or creating uncertainty. This type of manipulation can influence elections, destabilize political movements or undermine social cohesion.

A well-known example of the use of disinformation is the **accusation of Russian interference in the 2016 US presidential election.** It was alleged that Russian hackers and trolls deliberately spread disinformation to undermine confidence in the electoral system and deepen political divisions in the country. Such information wars are particularly difficult to combat because they are often conducted subtly and over a long period of time, making it difficult to clearly identify the source of the manipulation.

In addition to spreading disinformation, cyber warriors also use media attacks to disrupt or manipulate the communications of news agencies. A targeted cyber attack on major news portals could stop the dissemination of information or spread fake news, which could significantly weaken the public's trust in the media.

Information warfare can also be used in other ways to undermine the moral and psychological resilience of a population. By targeting **public opinion** and **perceptions of reality** , attackers can create deep social divisions, which can contribute to the destabilization of a country in the long term.

Conclusion on the potential targets in cyber warfare:

Cyberwar is a threat that goes far beyond classic military targets. It targets critical infrastructure, government institutions, military networks, financial systems and public opinion. The potential impact of such attacks is enormous and could cause not only short-term disruption but also long-term damage to a country's stability and security. The increasing reliance on digital networks makes modern societies vulnerable to cyberattacks and it is imperative that states and organizations develop robust protection measures to ward off these threats.

*

Strategies and Tactics in Cyber Warfare

Cyber warfare has given rise to a variety of strategies and tactics that differ greatly from traditional military approaches. While conventional wars are often characterized by physical force and open conflict, cyber wars often operate covertly and aim to manipulate, disrupt, or destroy digital infrastructures. The way cyber attacks are planned and carried out is of great strategic importance. This section examines both offensive and defensive approaches to cyber warfare, as well as asymmetric warfare and the use of deception.

Offensive Strategies: Disruption, Destruction and Espionage

Cyberattacks carried out as part of cyber warfare pursue various objectives, with the most common strategies aimed at disrupting or destroying systems or stealing information. Offensive strategies are often complex and require a high level of planning and technical expertise, as the attacks must be designed to effectively hit their targets while being as difficult to detect as possible.

One of the most common offensive strategies in cyber warfare is the **disruption of critical infrastructure** . This is often done through **denial-of-service (DoS)** or **distributed denial-of-service (DDoS) attacks** , in which networks are so overloaded by a flood of requests that they collapse. Such an attack can render websites, communication systems and other digital infrastructure unusable. It becomes particularly dangerous when such attacks target central infrastructure components such as the financial system, the power grid or the healthcare system, as the resulting outages can have devastating consequences for the civilian population.

In addition to disruption, **system destruction is also** an important tactic in cyber warfare. These attacks aim to permanently damage or destroy physical or digital infrastructures. A well-known example of such an attack is the aforementioned **Stuxnet worm** , which specifically sabotaged Iranian nuclear centrifuges by manipulating their control software, thereby causing physical damage to the facilities. Such attacks require a deep understanding of the target systems and precise planning to ensure that the damaging effects occur exactly as intended.

Cyber espionage is another common offensive tactic. It does not involve destroying systems, but rather secretly infiltrating networks to gather valuable information. This type of attack is particularly common in geopolitical conflicts, as governments seek to gain information about their opponents' military, economic, or political plans. One example of cyber espionage is the **APT29 (Advanced Persistent Threat 29) attack**, which was allegedly carried out by Russian intelligence services and targeted U.S. government agencies to steal classified information. Such attacks are often long-term and can go undetected for years, making them particularly dangerous.

Another offensive goal of cyberattacks can be the **manipulation of data** . Instead of simply stealing information, attackers can deliberately falsify or alter data. This can have devastating effects in many areas - from the financial world, where fake transactions or bookings could cause millions in losses, to military leadership, where manipulated data could lead to misjudgments and bad decisions.

Defense strategies: cyber defense, early warning systems and emergency management

In response to offensive cyberattacks, states and organizations are developing complex **defense strategies** to protect their digital infrastructures. Protection against cyberattacks requires constant vigilance, continuous improvement of security measures and a comprehensive strategy that includes both technological and organizational aspects.

One of the most basic defense strategies is **cyber defense.** This includes measures such as **firewalls, antivirus software** , and **intrusion detection systems (IDS)** that aim to detect and prevent malicious activity on networks. Such systems are designed to identify unusual traffic, monitor potential vulnerabilities, and report suspicious activity.

However, a robust defense system is only as effective as the ability to continually update it and keep it up to date with the latest technology, as attackers are constantly developing new methods to circumvent existing security measures.

In addition to reactive defenses, **early warning systems are** crucial to detecting attacks before they can cause damage. These systems analyze network anomalies and try to identify suspicious activity before it becomes a real threat. Modern early warning systems often use **artificial intelligence** and **machine learning** to automatically detect behavioral patterns that indicate an impending cyberattack. An example of such early warning systems is **behavioral analysis,** which examines unusual activities, such as a sudden increase in traffic or unauthorized access attempts.

An effective defense strategy also includes **emergency management,** which governs the response to a successful cyberattack. Even the best defense systems cannot always prevent attackers from succeeding, so it is critical to be prepared for the worst-case scenario. Emergency management strategies include **damage control plans** , such as immediately isolating infected systems, restoring backups, and quickly resuming operations. Additionally, teams must be able to forensically analyze the attack to identify the vulnerabilities that were exploited and prevent future attacks.

Asymmetric Warfare in Cyberspace: How Small Actors Can Attack Large Nations

One of the unique features of cyber warfare is the possibility of **asymmetric warfare** , in which relatively small or weak actors are able to attack more powerful opponents and inflict significant damage. Unlike traditional military conflicts, where military superiority often determines the outcome of a war, cyber wars can be fought by actors with limited resources.

An example of asymmetric warfare in cyberspace is **North Korea** , which has a highly sophisticated cyberwarfare capability despite its limited economic and military resources. In recent years, North Korea has been linked to a number of high-profile cyberattacks, including the **2014 Sony hack**, in which sensitive corporate data was stolen and released. This attack demonstrated that even a relatively small country is capable of causing significant damage to large corporations or even entire nations.

Non-state actors such as **cybercriminals** and **hacktivists also** exploit the asymmetric nature of cyberwarfare. These groups can often carry out attacks with minimal resources and little risk that have significant economic, political, or societal impact. A single hacker or small group of hackers can cause millions of dollars in damage or undermine public trust in institutions through the use of malware, phishing, or DDoS attacks.

Asymmetric warfare in cyberspace also presents opportunities for **terrorist groups** that could use digital attacks to cause economic damage or instill fear. Such groups may not have the resources to launch military attacks, but can inflict significant damage by using cyberattacks on critical infrastructure or financial systems.

The role of deception and false flags in cyber warfare:

Another crucial element in cyber warfare is **deception**. Cyberattacks provide attackers with the opportunity to conceal their true intentions or identity, making attribution of an attack—that is, identifying the real perpetrator—much more difficult. This uncertainty plays a central role in many attackers' strategy, as it allows them to carry out attacks without being held immediately accountable.

A particularly important deception tactic in cyberwarfare is the **false flag operation.** In this strategy, attackers carry out a cyberattack but make it appear as if it was carried out by another state or group. This can lead to diplomatic tensions, misunderstandings, or even military conflict if the victims of the attack blame the wrong actors for the attack.

A prominent example of the use of false flag operations was the **2017 NotPetya attack**, which was initially believed to be a run-of-the-mill ransomware attack aimed at financial gain. However, subsequent investigations revealed that the attack was **likely** initiated by state-sponsored hackers from Russia and aimed to destabilize the Ukrainian financial system. Disguising the attack as run-of-the-mill ransomware was a form of deception designed to obscure the true motives and those responsible.

The difficulty of clearly identifying attackers in cyberwarfare is a key advantage for states and groups that use deception. Many states have specialized **cyber intelligence units** that work to conceal the true identity of attackers or misrepresent them in order to hamper international investigations and avoid retaliation.

Conclusion on the strategies and tactics in cyber warfare:

Cyber warfare strategies and tactics are diverse and constantly evolving, as both attackers and defenders use new techniques and technologies to achieve their goals. While offensive cyber attacks aim to disrupt, destroy, and espionage, defensive strategies focus on repelling and mitigating damage. The asymmetric nature of cyber warfare also allows smaller actors to attack more powerful adversaries, making cyber warfare one of the most unpredictable and dangerous aspects of modern conflict. The use of deception and false flag operations adds another layer of complexity, as it makes attribution of attacks more difficult and can increase diplomatic tensions.

*

Ethics and Law in Cyberwar

The increasing importance of cyber warfare has raised a multitude of ethical and legal questions that are difficult to answer due to the intangible and often invisible nature of cyber attacks. While the international community has agreed on rules and laws governing warfare over centuries – such as the Geneva Conventions – there are still many grey areas in the field of cyber warfare. This section examines the ethical and legal challenges of cyber warfare and highlights the debate over its legitimacy and the difficulties of attribution.

International Cyberwar Legislation: Challenges and Gaps

In traditional laws of war, there are clear rules defining when a country may use military force, what is considered a legitimate target, and what actions are considered war crimes. These rules are largely set out in the **Geneva Conventions** and other international agreements governing the protection of civilians and the lawful use of force.

In the area of cyber warfare, however, there is currently no **comprehensive international legislation** that clearly defines the use of cyber weapons or the rules of cyber conflict. While there are efforts to apply principles of international law to cyber warfare, many details remain unclear. A central point in this debate is how cyber attacks should be treated in relation to existing definitions of violence and war.

The **UN Charter** states in Article 2(4) that the use or threat of force is prohibited in international relations, unless a country is acting in self-defense or as part of an operation authorized by the UN Security Council. The question, however, is whether a cyberattack can be considered "force" within the meaning of this article. A cyberattack can cause significant damage without using physical force. For example, an attack on a country's power grid could lead to chaos and possible loss of life even if no physical weapon is used.

Another problem is that cyberattacks often do not cause immediately visible damage, making it difficult to define them as an act of war. An attack that steals confidential data or disrupts military communications systems could be a form of espionage, but is rarely considered a direct attack. The line between **espionage, sabotage and direct attack** is often blurred in cyberwarfare, making it difficult to apply traditional laws of war.

Another area where there is a lack of clear regulations is the protection of **critical infrastructure.** In conventional wars, the laws of war prohibit targeted attacks on civilian infrastructure such as hospitals or water supplies. In cyber warfare, however, such infrastructure is often not adequately protected and there are no clear international rules regulating attacks on these facilities. This leads to an increased risk of civilian facilities becoming the target of cyber attacks, which could have potentially catastrophic consequences for the population.

The role of human rights in the digital space:

Another ethical issue that arises in the context of cyberwar is the protection of **human rights** in the digital space. The **right to privacy** , enshrined in the **Universal Declaration of Human Rights** and other international human rights treaties, is often violated in the digital space, especially through state-sponsored cyberattacks or espionage.

Cyberattacks aimed at stealing personal data or monitoring communications pose a direct threat to privacy. Many governments justify such attacks on the grounds of national security, but this often conflicts with the rights of the citizens affected. This is particularly problematic in authoritarian regimes that use cyber technologies to monitor their own populations and persecute opposition figures or dissidents.

Disinformation campaigns and **information warfare can** also violate human rights, particularly the **right to freedom of expression** and the **right to information** . When states deliberately spread false information or manipulate access to important information, people's ability to make informed decisions and express their opinions freely is severely compromised.

The question therefore arises as to how far the use of cyber technologies by states can go without violating fundamental human rights. This question is particularly difficult because there is often a conflict of interest between protecting national security and preserving individual freedoms. In many cases, the protection of privacy is sacrificed in favor of security, which has led to intense debates in democratic states.

The Problem of Attribution: How to Identify the Attacker

One of the biggest problems in cyber warfare is the **problem of attribution**, or how to clearly identify an attacker. Unlike physical attacks, where the attacker is usually clearly identifiable, cyber attacks can often be carried out anonymously. This is because attackers can easily cover their tracks by operating across different servers and networks or using **false identities** to conceal their true intentions.

This **invisibility** not only makes it harder to defend against cyberattacks, but also poses a serious challenge to enforcing international law. If a state or organization cannot say with certainty who is responsible for an attack, it is difficult to take countermeasures or hold the perpetrator accountable. In many cases, it takes months or even years for the identity of the attacker to be revealed - if at all.

Another factor that complicates attribution is the possibility of **false flag operations,** where an attacker makes it appear as if the attack came from another state or group. Such operations can exacerbate geopolitical tensions and lead to diplomatic or military misjudgments if one country falsely blames another state for an attack. This could trigger a **spiral of escalation** that is difficult to control.

To improve attribution, many countries have started to set up specialized **cyber intelligence units** that specialize in identifying attackers. These units use advanced analytical techniques and forensic methods to trace the traces of cyber attacks and determine the origin of the attacks. However, despite these efforts, attribution remains one of the biggest challenges in cyber warfare as attackers are constantly developing new techniques to conceal their tracks.

The debate about the "legitimacy" of cyber attacks as a means of warfare:

Another key ethical and legal issue in cyber warfare is the question of the **legitimacy of cyber attacks** as a means of warfare. In traditional wars, attacks on military targets are permitted under international law as long as they comply with the principles of proportionality and the distinction between civilian and military targets. But in cyber warfare, it is often difficult to distinguish between civilian and military targets, as many of the systems attacked are used for both civilian and military purposes.

An example of this is **dual-purpose infrastructure**, such as a country's electricity grid or communications system. These infrastructures are often crucial for military operations, but at the same time are essential to the daily lives of civilians. An attack on a country's electricity grid could therefore have both military and civilian implications, raising the question of whether such an attack can be considered a legitimate military act.

Another ethical dilemma is the **proportionality** of cyber attacks. International law requires that military action be proportionate to the expected military benefits. However, in cyber warfare, it is often difficult to estimate what impact an attack will have. An attack targeting a military communications network could have unintended consequences on civilian infrastructure, which could call into question the proportionality of the attack.

In addition, there is the question of whether cyberattacks that do not cause **physical damage** should be considered legitimate acts of war. Cyberattacks that simply steal data or disrupt networks might be considered less serious than physical attacks. However, even such attacks can have a significant impact on a country's national security and economic stability, which is why some experts argue that cyberattacks should be regulated as strictly as conventional acts of war.

Another issue in the debate about the legitimacy of cyberattacks is the **civilian harm** that can be caused by such attacks. Since many cyberattacks specifically target critical infrastructure that is also used by civilians, there is a high risk that the civilian population will be indirectly drawn into the conflict. This raises the question of the extent to which cyberattacks are compatible with the principle of protecting civilians enshrined in the laws of war.

Conclusion on the ethical and legal aspects of cyber warfare:
The ethical and legal issues arising from cyber warfare are complex and multifaceted. The invisibility and anonymity of cyber attacks, the difficulty of attribution and the lack of international legislation make it difficult to formulate clear rules for the use of cyber weapons. At the same time, cyber wars pose a significant threat to human rights, privacy and the security of civilians. The international community is faced with the challenge of finding ways to regulate the use of cyber weapons and ensure that the digital space does not become an uncontrolled battlefield.

The role of intelligence services and cyber intelligence:
In the age of cyber warfare, intelligence agencies play a crucial role in reconnaissance, defense, and conducting cyber operations. The digitization of communications and information systems has opened up new opportunities for intelligence agencies to respond to potential threats, collect intelligence, and monitor adversary activities. Cyber intelligence has become an indispensable part of modern conflicts, both in preventive defense and in conducting offensive operations. This section examines the role of intelligence and cyber intelligence in detail and shows how modern technologies are used to collect intelligence and prevent cyber attacks.

How intelligence services collect and use information in the digital space:
Intelligence agencies have traditionally specialized in gathering information about potential threats, analyzing it, and then developing measures to defend against or respond to those threats. In the digital

age, the focus of intelligence work has expanded to include **cyberspace** . Digital networks, encrypted communications, and large amounts of data present both challenges and opportunities for intelligence agencies.

One of the main tasks of intelligence agencies in cyber intelligence is to **intercept and monitor communications.** With the advent of digitalization, most global communications are conducted over digital networks, giving intelligence agencies the ability to collect massive amounts of data. This includes both **public** and **private communications** , such as emails, phone calls, messaging services, and social networks. A prominent example of the expansion of surveillance in the digital space is the **Prism program** of the **National Security Agency (NSA)** in the USA, which became known when Edward Snowden leaked information about it in 2013. This program allowed the NSA to gain direct access to the data of major technology companies, including Google, Facebook, and Apple, to collect information about potential threats.

In addition to monitoring communications, intelligence agencies also use **hacking** and other offensive cyber methods to gain access to confidential information. This type of cyber intelligence is often referred to as **active cyber intelligence** , as it is usually associated with penetrating foreign networks. The purpose of such operations is to gather intelligence about the military, economic, or political plans of adversaries without being detected. An example of such activities are the **attacks by the APT29 (Advanced Persistent Threat 29) group** , also known as "Cozy Bear," which is associated with Russian intelligence services. This group has carried out numerous cyber espionage attacks on Western governments and institutions to steal sensitive information.

Interception of satellite communications is also an important component of cyber intelligence. Many military and diplomatic communication channels use satellites to transmit information securely. Intelligence agencies have special units that specialize in intercepting and decrypting such signals to gain access to confidential information. The technology needed to do this is highly sophisticated, but many states invest significant resources in this type of surveillance because it provides valuable insight into the activities of their adversaries.

Cyber awareness as a preventive measure:
Preventive **cyber intelligence** plays a key role in preventing cyber attacks. Intelligence agencies continuously work to detect threats early, before they can actually be implemented. By gathering information about potential attackers and their tactics, techniques and procedures (TTPs), defensive measures can be taken in a timely manner to prevent or mitigate impending attacks.

A key part of preventive cyber intelligence is **monitoring darknet forums and criminal networks**, where hackers and cybercriminals often share information or plan attacks. Intelligence agencies infiltrate such networks to gain insight into planned attacks, the sale of vulnerabilities, or the sharing of malware. This information is then used to identify and close vulnerabilities in their own systems before they can be exploited by attackers.

Another aspect of preventive cyber intelligence is the **analysis of threat data.** Intelligence agencies work with **threat intelligence platforms** that collect and analyze large amounts of data about past cyber attacks and current threats. By examining **pattern recognition, behavioral analysis**, and **anomalies** in networks, potential attacks can often be detected early. Modern systems increasingly use **artificial intelligence (AI)** and **machine learning** to automatically identify threats and initiate defense measures. These technologies are particularly useful for detecting so-called **zero-day attacks** - attacks that target previously unknown vulnerabilities.

Cooperation between intelligence agencies and the **private sector** is another key element of preventive cyber intelligence. Companies, especially those operating in critical infrastructure such as energy suppliers or banks, work closely with intelligence agencies to exchange information about potential threats. These **public-private partnerships** enable both sides to be better prepared for cyber threats and to jointly develop protective measures.

The importance of data analysis and big data in intelligence:

With the rapid increase in digital communication and the interconnectedness of systems, **data analysis has** become a central part of modern cyber intelligence. Intelligence agencies are faced with huge amounts of information that need to be analyzed. This includes not only communication data, but also **metadata, behavioral patterns** and **technical information** about networks and systems.

Big data technologies play a key role in managing these volumes of data. By analyzing large and complex data sets, intelligence agencies can identify potential threats that might be missed in smaller data sets. **Machine learning** enables intelligence units to identify patterns and trends that could indicate an impending attack or the activities of a particular hacker group.

One example of the successful use of big data in cyber intelligence is the **XKeyscore project,** which also became known through Edward Snowden's revelations. This program allows the NSA to search almost every form of internet communication and create detailed profiles of people who are classified as potential threats. However, such systems are not without controversy, as they often stand in the tension between national security and the protection of privacy.

In addition to identifying threats, data analysis is also used to study the **behavior of cybercriminals and hacker groups** . By analyzing previous attacks, intelligence agencies can determine which tactics and techniques certain groups prefer and develop defense strategies accordingly. This type of **behavioral analysis** is particularly useful for detecting repeated attacks by a particular group and predicting their tactics.

Intelligence operations and espionage through cyber attacks:

While intelligence agencies often work defensively to protect their own networks and ward off threats, they also conduct **offensive**

operations aimed at stealing information from hostile states or organizations. **Cyber espionage** is one of the most important tasks of modern intelligence agencies, as it allows access to information that is crucial to military, political or economic decisions.

Cyber espionage operations are usually well planned and can be carried out over long periods of time without victims becoming aware of them. Attackers often use **advanced persistent threats (APTs)** to penetrate networks and remain undetected while continuously gathering information. This type of attack is particularly difficult to detect because attackers deliberately use unobtrusive ways to gain access to networks and remain active there for long periods of time.

A famous example of cyber espionage is the 2015 **hack of** the U.S. government's Office of Personnel Management (OPM), in which attackers believed to be linked to China stole millions of sensitive data on U.S. government employees, including security clearances and other confidential information. This information could be used to blackmail U.S. officials or exploit vulnerabilities in the U.S. government.

In addition to gathering information through cyberattacks, intelligence agencies also use **disinformation campaigns** and **psychological operations** to influence public opinion or promote political instability. These types of operations aim to undermine trust in institutions, damage the credibility of governments, or destabilize geopolitical opponents. Disinformation campaigns are usually difficult to detect and can be spread through social media and other digital channels.

Conclusion on the role of intelligence services and cyber intelligence:

Intelligence and cyber intelligence play a central role in modern warfare and in preventing cyber attacks. The ability to collect, analyze and respond to information in the digital space is critical to success in cyber warfare. At the same time, the massive amount of data and complex technologies used in cyber intelligence present both opportunities and challenges. The constant evolution of attack methods requires intelligence agencies to continuously adapt their tactics and technologies in order to respond effectively to the changing threats.

*

Cyberwar and the Private Sector

The role of the private sector in cyber warfare is becoming increasingly important as companies around the world are increasingly becoming targets of cyberattacks. While states are typically at the center of cyber conflicts, the business sector is often directly affected, with numerous cyberattacks specifically targeting companies, especially those holding critical infrastructure or valuable data. Companies are challenged to protect themselves against a variety of threats, including industrial espionage, sabotage, and financial extortion through ransomware. This section examines the role of the private sector in cyber warfare, the growing challenges of cybersecurity, and collaboration between companies and state actors.

Attacks on companies: industrial espionage, data theft and sabotage

In the globally connected economy, companies are a prime target for cyberattacks. Sectors that process large amounts of confidential or valuable information, such as the **financial sector**, the **technology sector** and the **healthcare sector, are particularly affected.** Attacks on companies can have catastrophic consequences, both for the company itself and for the economy of an entire country.

A key motive for cyberattacks on companies is **industrial espionage**. States and non-state actors, such as well-organized hacker groups, often try to steal confidential company data in order to gain a competitive advantage. In practice, this often means the theft of **intellectual property,** such as **research results, technologies** or **production secrets.** A well-known example of industrial espionage is the **attack on Sony Pictures Entertainment in 2014,** in which confidential data and films were stolen and released. It was suspected that North Korea was behind this attack, as the attack was linked to a film that criticized the North Korean regime.

POSSIBILITIES OF CYBERWARS

Another common target of cyberattacks on companies is the **theft of customer data** . Companies that store personal information of millions of customers, such as banks, retailers or hospitals, are a lucrative target for cybercriminals. An attack on these databases can lead to **identity theft, fraud** or **extortion** . A serious incident occurred in 2017 when **Equifax** , one of the largest credit agencies in the United States, fell victim to a massive data theft in which the personal information of approximately 147 million people was compromised.

In addition to espionage and data theft, companies are increasingly facing **sabotage attacks** . Such attacks aim to disrupt operations or sabotage important systems in order to paralyze the company. **Ransomware attacks** are a particularly widespread form of sabotage, in which hackers encrypt a company's systems and only release them in return for a ransom payment. One example is the **2017 WannaCry attack** , which affected thousands of companies and organizations worldwide, including hospitals, which were forced to postpone operations and treatments.

The role of private security companies in cyber defense:

The increase in cyberattacks on businesses has greatly increased the demand for **cybersecurity solutions** . Private security companies play a central role in protecting businesses and organizations against cyber threats. These companies offer a variety of **services** , including **network security solutions, employee training** , and **incident response teams** that can intervene immediately in the event of an attack to limit the damage.

Private cybersecurity companies often work closely with governments and state security agencies to detect and respond to threats early. Many of these companies have highly specialized teams that are familiar with the latest technologies and attack techniques and can respond quickly to new threats. An example of such a company is **FireEye** , which has become known worldwide for its extensive threat analysis and detection of state-sponsored cyberattacks.

A key aspect of the work of private security companies is **incident response**. When a company becomes the target of a cyberattack, a quick and coordinated response is crucial to limit the damage. Incident response teams take control of the situation, analyze the attack, isolate affected systems, and restore operations as quickly as possible. These teams often specialize in repelling **ransomware attacks**, stopping **data leaks**, or mitigating **DDoS attacks**.

In addition to directly preventing attacks, private security companies also help companies to be better prepared for future threats. This is often done through **security audits**, which review a company's existing security systems and identify vulnerabilities. In addition, many companies offer training for employees to raise awareness of cyber threats and ensure that employees do not inadvertently contribute to attacks, for example through phishing or weak passwords.

Cooperation between governments and companies in the field of cybersecurity:

Because cyberattacks often have global implications and affect both state and non-state actors, cooperation between **governments and companies** in the field of cybersecurity has increased significantly in recent years. These **public-private partnerships** are necessary to share information about threats, work together to defend against attacks, and combat global cyber threats.

One example of this cooperation is the establishment of **cyber defence centres**, in which government authorities and private companies work closely together to monitor threats in real time and respond to attacks. In the US, the **Cybersecurity and Infrastructure Security Agency (CISA) works** closely with companies that operate critical infrastructure to identify potential threats and develop countermeasures. Similar initiatives also exist in Europe, for example within the framework of the **European Network and Information Security Agency (ENISA)**.

Cooperation between governments and businesses also includes **sharing threat intelligence.** Since government intelligence agencies often have extensive data on potential threats, it is crucial for businesses to be informed early about potential attacks. Such information can help close security gaps and prepare for impending attacks. At the same time, government agencies receive important information about cyber incidents from businesses that can be used to further improve the national cybersecurity strategy.

Another important area of cooperation is **cybersecurity research and development.** Governments and companies are increasingly investing in the development of new technologies to improve **resilience** against cyberattacks. This includes research into new encryption technologies, developing **artificial intelligence (AI)** for threat detection and promoting quantum computing to meet future security requirements.

Economic consequences of cyber attacks on global markets:

Cyberattacks on companies not only have a direct impact on the organizations affected, but also on **global markets.** A successful cyberattack can lead to **massive financial losses** , shake investor confidence and threaten the stability of entire industries. Such an incident can destabilize markets and have far-reaching economic consequences.

An example of the economic impact of cyberattacks is the attack on **Bangladesh's financial system in 2016,** where hackers managed to steal over $80 million from the central bank. This attack sparked global concern about the security of financial institutions and led to banks worldwide strengthening their security measures.

Stock **exchanges** are particularly vulnerable to cyberattacks because trading takes place in a matter of seconds and a disruption or manipulation of trading could cause significant losses. A targeted attack on a stock exchange could lead to a **massive sell-off of stocks** and plunge entire economies into crisis. Even minor disruptions or the mere suspicion of a security breach can shake investor confidence and lead to share price losses.

Another important aspect is **supply chains**, which are closely linked in the modern economy. A cyberattack on one company can impact entire supply chains, especially in industries such as the **automotive** or **pharmaceutical industries**, where many companies work closely together. An attack on one company can lead to production delays and delivery bottlenecks, which in turn affects the affected company's business partners.

The economic consequences of cyberattacks are often difficult to quantify, as they go far beyond the direct costs. In addition to the financial losses from stolen data or ransom payments, companies also have to contend with **reputational damage** that can affect customer trust in the long term. The impact is particularly severe for companies that manage personal data, as such incidents can undermine confidence in their ability to protect data.

Conclusion on the role of the private sector in cyber warfare:

Businesses play a central role in modern cyber warfare as they are increasingly targeted by cyberattacks that can have both economic and security implications. Collaboration between the private sector and government actors is critical to building cyber resilience and protecting global markets from the economic consequences of such attacks. As cyber threats continue to grow, businesses must continually invest in improving their security measures and work closely with governments to defend against the ever-evolving cyber threats.

*

The Psychology of Cyberwar

In addition to the physical and technological aspects, **psychology plays** a central role in cyber warfare. Cyberattacks and disinformation campaigns target not only infrastructure and data, but also the consciousness and emotions of individuals and societies. Fear, uncertainty and mistrust can be used as powerful weapons in digital conflicts to incite panic, undermine trust and create instability. This section highlights the psychological mechanisms used in cyber warfare, as well as the impact of social engineering, disinformation and propaganda on collective consciousness and trust in technology.

The role of fear, uncertainty and mistrust in cyber warfare:

Cyberwarfare often uses **psychological tactics** to create uncertainty and fear. Unlike physical attacks, which cause visible and tangible damage, the effects of cyberattacks are often less obvious, which can increase the sense of threat. The invisibility and complexity of cyberattacks leads to a constant feeling of **vulnerability** , both among individuals and among governments and companies.

A key factor that amplifies the psychological impact of cyberattacks is **uncertainty about the attacker.** Since it is often difficult to immediately identify the origin of a cyberattack, victims do not know who the attacker is, what their goals are, and whether further attacks are to be expected. This uncertainty can lead to a deep sense of **distrust** - both towards technology and towards the institutions responsible for protecting digital infrastructures.

Spreading **fear** is one of the most effective psychological weapons in cyber warfare. Attackers can create **fear of further attacks** or of the threat escalating. A well-known example is the **NotPetya attack of 2017** , where malware spread rapidly and brought down computer systems worldwide. Although the attackers may have had only a specific target in mind, the rapid spread of the malware led to global panic and a feeling that no one was safe.

Ransomware attacks also use fear as a means to control their victims. The threat of permanently encrypting or publishing important data creates psychological pressure that often forces companies and individuals to pay ransoms, even if there is no guarantee that the data will actually be recovered.

In addition, **media coverage plays** a large role in amplifying the psychological impact of cyberattacks. News of successful cyberattacks, especially on high-profile targets such as governments, banks or hospitals, increases the feeling of insecurity among the population. This often leads to people losing confidence in the security of technology and in the ability of their government or institutions to protect them from such attacks.

Psychological warfare through disinformation and propaganda:

Disinformation is a powerful weapon of psychological warfare in cyberspace. Cyber warriors deliberately use false or misleading information to influence public opinion, promote political instability or undermine trust in institutions. Such **information wars** aim to manipulate people's consciousness and create deep societal divisions.

A prominent example of the use of disinformation is **election interference.** By using bots and fake social media accounts, attackers spread deliberately false information to undermine voters' trust in the electoral system or discredit specific political candidates. The **allegation of Russian interference in the 2016 US presidential election** shows how disinformation can be used to foment political unrest and undermine trust in democratic institutions. By spreading false news and misleading information on social media, attackers were able to undermine public confidence in the integrity of the election while exacerbating existing political tensions.

Another important element of psychological warfare is **propaganda** , which aims to influence public perception and gain support for specific political goals or ideologies. In the digital age, propaganda has proliferated on **social media** and **online platforms** , where it is posted in the form of memes, videos, and fake news articles. The speed and reach with which disinformation can spread on social media makes it a powerful tool for influencing entire populations.

Cyberwarriors also use disinformation and propaganda to deepen **societal divisions** . By spreading content that reinforces existing lines of conflict, such as **ethnic, religious or political differences** , they can escalate tensions in society. This tactic leads to a polarization of the population and makes it difficult for the affected states to maintain political stability. This type of psychological warfare has long-term effects, as it undermines citizens' trust in their fellow human beings, in the media and in the government.

Social Engineering: Manipulation of Individuals and Organizations

Social engineering is another effective method of psychological warfare in cyberspace, where people are deliberately manipulated to gain access to confidential information or to perform certain actions. Instead of exploiting technical vulnerabilities in computer systems, social engineering focuses on exploiting **human vulnerabilities** - such as the trust, ignorance or fear of victims.

One of the most common forms of social engineering is **phishing**, in which attackers use fake emails or messages to trick users into revealing sensitive information, such as passwords or credit card details. Phishing attacks are particularly successful because they use psychological tactics such as **urgency, fear** , or **trust** to get victims to respond to the fraudulent messages. One example is **spear phishing,** in which attackers specifically target high-ranking employees of a company or government to gain access to sensitive data.

CEO fraud is another form of social engineering in which hackers impersonate high-ranking executives of a company and trick employees into transferring large sums of money into fraudulent accounts. These attacks rely on the authority and trust that a leader enjoys in an organization. By manipulating and creating urgency, attackers are able to get victims to take actions that they would not normally take.

Social engineering is particularly dangerous because it is often difficult to detect and is based on psychological mechanisms deeply rooted in human nature. Many people are unaware of how easily they can be manipulated, and even tech-savvy users can fall victim to such attacks if they are pressured or not sufficiently vigilant.

Impact of cyberwar on collective consciousness and trust in technology:

The psychological impact of cyberwar goes far beyond the immediate consequences of attacks. They have the potential to profoundly change **collective consciousness** and **trust in technology**. Cyberattacks on critical infrastructure or the targeted spread of disinformation can shake people's trust in the stability of their society and in the security of technologies.

One of the most serious impacts is the loss of **trust in digital systems.** When people feel that their personal data is not secure or that their communications are being monitored, it leads to a general distrust of technology. This can affect **usage behavior**, as people may be hesitant to use digital services or conduct online transactions for fear of becoming a victim of a cyberattack.

In addition, cyberwarfare can undermine trust in **government institutions** and **democratic processes** . When attacks on electoral systems, government institutions or public services are successful, citizens begin to doubt their government's ability to protect them. This leads to increasing **polarization** and a sense of **helplessness** that is dangerous for the stability of democracies.

Another long-term problem is the **sense of constant threat** created by the invisibility and unpredictability of cyberattacks. The idea that attacks can happen anywhere, anytime, without immediate notice can lead to a **collective fear**. This fear, in turn, can undermine trust in society as a whole and affect the mental health of the population.

Conclusion on the psychology of cyberwar:

The psychological dimensions of cyber warfare are a critical factor in the success of modern cyber attacks. By deliberately manipulating fear, uncertainty and mistrust, attackers can achieve profound societal and political impacts that extend far beyond the actual attack. Disinformation, propaganda and social engineering are powerful tools of psychological warfare aimed at undermining trust in technology, institutions and social stability. To counter these threats, societies must develop not only technological but also psychological defense strategies to build resilience against the psychological effects of cyber warfare.

*

The Future of Cyberwar

Cyber warfare is constantly evolving, driven by technological advances and changing geopolitical realities. While states and non-state actors have already entered the battlefield of cyberspace, there are strong indications that future warfare in digital space will become even more complex and dangerous. New technologies such as **quantum computers, autonomous weapons systems and artificial intelligence (AI)** will have the potential to fundamentally change the way cyber warfare is fought. At the same time, the international community will be challenged to create new sets of rules and cooperation to prevent the escalation of cyber conflicts. This section examines the possible future developments in cyber warfare and the role that international cooperation could play.

Possible future developments in cyber warfare:

One of the most exciting and threatening technological advances that could shape cyber warfare in the future is the development of **quantum computers.** While today's computers are based on binary systems in which information is stored as ones and zeros, a quantum computer works on the basis of **qubits**, which can occupy multiple states simultaneously. This enables quantum computers to process enormous amounts of data in a fraction of the time that classical computers need.

The use of quantum computers in cyber warfare could bring about critical changes both offensively and defensively. On the **offensive side,** quantum computers could be able to crack complex **encryptions** that are currently considered secure. This could allow attackers to infiltrate even the most well-protected systems and steal or tamper with confidential information. A **quantum attack,** for example, could put the entire financial industry at risk by intercepting transactions or compromising databases. There are fears that attackers could be able to overcome **military communications networks**, which are currently protected by strong encryption, within minutes.

On the **defensive side,** however, quantum computers could also help improve cybersecurity. With the development of **quantum cryptography** , based on the laws of quantum physics, systems could be created that are theoretically unbreakable. This type of cryptography would allow information to be transmitted in such a way that any form of interception would be immediately detected. This would allow states and companies to protect their sensitive data from the cyberattacks of the future. The challenge will be whether these security measures can be put into practice before quantum computers are available.

Autonomous weapon systems are another potential threat that could shape the future of cyber warfare. These systems are based on **artificial intelligence (AI)** and can make decisions without human intervention. Autonomous weapon systems are already in use in conventional warfare in the form of **drones** and **robotic weapon systems** , but they could play an even more far-reaching role in cyber warfare. Autonomous cyber weapons could be programmed to independently search for vulnerabilities in enemy networks and launch attacks without a human operator being directly involved. Such **autonomous cyber attacks** would be particularly difficult to defend against because they would be able to dynamically adapt to the enemy's defense strategies.

An example of the potential use of autonomous systems in cyber warfare could be an **AI-driven attack system** that uses machine learning to constantly identify new vulnerabilities in a network and is able to launch attacks that immediately respond to the discovered gaps. This would drastically reduce attackers' response time and put defenders in a difficult position, as human cybersecurity teams would often not be able to respond as quickly.

Another scenario could be the use of **swarm intelligence** in cyber warfare, where many small, networked attack programs act as a "swarm" to infiltrate a target. These swarms could automatically adapt to new environments and use collective decision-making to seek out and exploit vulnerabilities in a network. Such systems could be particularly effective when targeting **critical infrastructure** , as they would be able to attack multiple parts of a system simultaneously, rendering it unusable.

Artificial intelligence (AI) itself will play an increasingly large role in cyber warfare, both offensively and defensively. AI-powered systems will increasingly be used to analyze large amounts of **threat data and identify patterns in attacks that human analysts may miss. This can help improve early warning systems** that detect attacks before they can cause serious damage. Another use of AI is to automate **incident response** . AI systems could respond to attacks autonomously, for example by isolating affected systems, blocking attackers, or closing vulnerabilities without the need for human intervention.

On the **offensive side** , AI could be used to launch highly **adaptive attacks** that autonomously adapt to the enemy's defense systems during the attack. Such **intelligent attacks** could not only overcome human reaction times, but also exploit vulnerabilities that are previously unknown. An example would be AI-powered malware that is able to modify and optimize its own attack techniques while penetrating a network.

International cooperation to prevent escalation in cyber warfare:

As technologies evolve, international cooperation will be critical in regulating and controlling cyber warfare. Without international rules and agreements, there is a risk of **uncontrolled escalation** of cyber conflicts that could lead to widespread destruction without the use of physical force.

A first step towards creating an **international framework for cyberwar** is the establishment of norms and agreements that regulate the use of cyber weapons. The international community has made successful agreements on the use of weapons of mass destruction in the past, but there is still no comprehensive international treaty that specifically addresses cyberwarfare. States could, for example, **agree on rules to**

prevent attacks on critical infrastructure, especially those essential to providing civilians with electricity, water, and medical care.

Establishing **trust measures** between states is another important aspect. Countries should develop mechanisms to enable **transparent communication in the event of cyberattacks** to avoid misunderstandings. In a traditional military conflict, diplomatic channels can be used to prevent escalations, but in cyberwar, the ability to quickly identify the real attacker is often lacking. This can lead to **miscalculations** and unwanted counterattacks that further aggravate the situation.

There are already **regional initiatives** to promote cooperation in the field of cybersecurity. For example, the European Union has launched the **EU Network and Information Security Directive (NIS Directive)**, **which provides for closer cooperation between EU member states in defending against cyberattacks. In addition, NATO is working on developing cyber defense strategies** that will enable member states to respond jointly in the event of a cyberattack.

Another important issue in international cooperation is **combating the attribution** of cyberattacks. Since **anonymity** is a central feature of many cyberattacks, it will be crucial for the international community to develop **standards for forensics** and **techniques for identifying attackers**. This would make it easier for countries to hold those responsible to account and take countermeasures without relying on vague suspicions.

The role of diplomacy and cyber diplomacy:

A key aspect of international cooperation is **cyber diplomacy** – the use of diplomatic channels to prevent the escalation of cyber conflicts and to create common rules. In recent years, many countries have appointed specialized **cyber ambassadors** who work to conclude international agreements and build trust between states.

The **United Nations (UN)** plays an important role in this. The UN has established working groups to address **international cybersecurity**

issues and seek to develop guidelines that govern the use of cyber weapons. A key part of these efforts is the creation of **confidence-building measures** to ensure that cyber conflicts do not escalate and that states have clear lines of communication to avoid misunderstandings.

In addition, an **international cyber convention could** be created that regulates the use of cyber weapons in a similar way to the Geneva Conventions for conventional weapons. Such regulations could prohibit attacks on civilian infrastructure and provide for sanctions against states that carry out or support cyber attacks. This would also help states that adhere to these rules to have more confidence in the security of global cyberspace.

Conclusion on the future of cyber warfare:

The future of cyber warfare will depend heavily on technological advances and international cooperation. While quantum computers, autonomous weapons systems and artificial intelligence have the potential to radically change the way cyberattacks are conducted, it will be crucial that the international community develops rules and norms to prevent uncontrolled escalation of cyber conflict. Digital space is increasingly becoming a central arena of geopolitical disputes, and states must learn to use both technological and diplomatic means to ensure peace and security in cyberspace.

*

"Military Cyberwars and Their Dangers for the Affected Population"

Definition and Delimitation of Military Cyberwar

Military cyber warfare has become a central element of modern warfare in recent decades. While wars have traditionally been fought on physical battlefields with conventional weapons, cyber warfare has established itself as a new, invisible front. The term "cyber warfare" refers to the use of information and communication technologies to damage or destabilize enemy military and civilian infrastructures. In contrast to conventional conflicts, cyber warfare takes place in virtual space and aims to exploit vulnerabilities through the use of computers, networks and software in order to gain strategic advantages.

Cyberwarfare is typically a form of asymmetric warfare in which a nation or group seeks to weaken a more powerful military force without engaging in direct military confrontation. This is particularly relevant in an age where modern states are increasingly dependent on digital networks to operate their infrastructure. Through cyberattacks, hostile actors can disrupt or even completely paralyze energy supplies, communications networks, financial systems, and military control systems.

Military cyber warfare is to be distinguished from non-military cyber attacks or criminal activities such as hacking or data theft. While these forms of cyber attacks can also cause serious damage, military cyber operations primarily aim to alter the balance of power between nations. In military conflicts, cyber warfare is often seen as a complement to traditional military means, offering the ability to disrupt an opponent's operations without conducting a physical attack.

The line between traditional wars and cyberwars is often blurred, as in many cases cyberattacks are used as part of a broader military conflict. For example, cyberattacks might be conducted in preparation for a ground offensive to weaken the enemy's communications and defense systems. In other cases, cyberwar might be fought on its own to achieve political or economic goals without the need for traditional military action.

A well-known example of the use of cyber warfare is the "Stuxnet" attack, considered by many to be one of the first confirmed cyberattacks on critical infrastructure. Stuxnet, a sophisticated computer virus, was used to disrupt Iran's nuclear program. This attack aimed to secretly sabotage the centrifuges used for uranium enrichment. This caused significant delays in Iran's nuclear program without a single shot being fired. This incident highlighted the potential power of cyberattacks and their ability to influence the balance of power between states.

In a military context, cyber warfare has several advantages. First, it offers actors the ability to conduct attacks without being physically present. This means that nations can launch cyberattacks remotely, making it more difficult to identify or punish the attackers. In addition, cyberattacks can usually be carried out at a relatively low cost, especially compared to conventional military operations that require significant resources. This makes cyberwarfare particularly attractive to states or organizations with limited military capabilities.

Another characteristic of cyberwar is its invisibility. While traditional wars leave physical destruction in their wake, the damage of cyberwar is often not immediately visible. While data manipulation, system failures, or the theft of sensitive information can have long-term and profound effects, they are usually not as obvious as destruction caused by bombs or missiles. This can lead to confusion and make it difficult for victims to respond quickly and effectively to attacks.

Over the past few years, it has become clear that cyberwars are not only taking place between states, but that non-state actors also play an important role. Hacker groups such as **"Anonymous"** or the Russian group **"Fancy Bear"** have shown that private actors are also capable of carrying out sophisticated cyberattacks that can rival the capabilities of state actors. These non-state actors often operate in secret and have no clear ties to governments, making it even more difficult to identify them or hold them accountable for their attacks.

Despite the immense threat posed by military cyber warfare, there is still a lack of clear international regulations and laws governing the use of cyber weapons worldwide. While there are a number of initiatives and conventions aimed at prohibiting cyber attacks on critical infrastructure, many of these agreements are difficult to enforce and are often ignored. This leads to a kind of "wild west" in cyberspace, where states and non-state actors make their own rules.

With the rise of cyber warfare, there has also been an increased militarization of cyberspace. Nations such as the United States, China, and Russia have invested significant resources in developing cyber defense and cyber attack capabilities. Cyber troops and commands have been integrated into the military structure, and there are signs that cyber attacks will play an even greater role in future conflicts. In this context, the question is how far states are willing to accept cyber warfare as a legitimate means of warfare and what impact this will have on the global security situation.

Cyberwar can have serious political and economic consequences. Not only can it destabilize governments, but it can also strain international relations and disrupt trade. In a world that is increasingly interconnected, a large-scale cyberwar can have far-reaching consequences that extend far beyond the nations immediately affected. The uncertainty and distrust created by such attacks could lead to an escalation that could ultimately result in physical conflict.

Overall, military cyber warfare has established itself as a new battlefield that challenges many of the conventional rules and norms of warfare. While cyber wars potentially result in fewer direct casualties than traditional military conflicts, they still pose enormous risks to the societies involved and to global stability. The constant evolution of technologies and the increasing reliance on digital networks mean that the threat of cyber warfare will continue to grow in the coming years.

Technological Mechanisms and Strategies of Cyber Warfare

Technological mechanisms play a central role in military cyber warfare. The strategies used are diverse and constantly adapt to the rapid developments in information technology. Cyber weapons used in military conflicts differ fundamentally from traditional weapons because they do not physically destroy, but rather exploit vulnerabilities in computer systems, networks and infrastructures. A wide range of tools and techniques are used, which vary depending on the target and intended effect.

Some of the most common cyber weapons include viruses, worms, malware, ransomware, distributed denial of service (DDoS) attacks, and zero-day exploits. Each of these technologies has a specific way of working, but the common goal is to disrupt, tamper with, or completely control a computer system. A virus attack aims to infiltrate a computer system by spreading malicious code that either steals information or disables the system. Worms, on the other hand, spread independently across networks and can infect large parts of a system without the need for human intervention.

One of the most serious attacks in cyber warfare is the use of zero-day exploits. These attacks take advantage of unknown vulnerabilities in software or systems before developers have a chance to release patches or updates to fix them. This means that even the best security measures can be ineffective because the vulnerability being exploited was not known. Zero-day exploits are particularly valuable and rare, making them a key tool in cyber warfare.

DDoS attacks, which aim to paralyze servers by flooding them with requests, are also one of the preferred methods of taking down websites, networks and other online services. This form of attack often leads to widespread disruptions in critical infrastructures, such as banks, government agencies or communications services. A massive DDoS attack can even paralyze a state's defense systems, leading to a complete disruption of public and military life.

Another important element of cyber warfare is data manipulation. Attacks aimed at stealing, altering or destroying data can have devastating effects. In military contexts, changing orders, manipulating communications data or gaining access to classified information can compromise an adversary's entire war strategy. In Ukraine, for example, attacks were reported in 2017 in which Russian hackers attempted to disrupt the military's communications systems and transmit false information to create confusion and impair coordination of defense efforts.

In addition to these more offensive techniques, there are also numerous defensive mechanisms that states use to protect their systems against cyberattacks. Cyber defense systems use encryption, firewalls, intrusion detection systems and artificial intelligence to detect and ward off threats. As these technologies become more advanced, attackers are also constantly looking for new ways to circumvent these protections. Therefore, military cyber warfare is a constant race between attackers and defenders, with the side that is one step ahead technologically having the advantage.

One particularly innovative area of cyber warfare is the use of artificial intelligence (AI) and machine learning. AI-powered systems can be used to identify potential vulnerabilities in real time, analyze attacks, and take appropriate countermeasures. On the other hand, attackers can use AI to carry out more targeted and efficient attacks. For example, an AI-driven attack could automatically identify vulnerabilities while maximizing its chances of success by constantly adapting to the target's defenses.

A notable example of the use of cyber weapons in military conflict was the attack on Estonia in 2007. At that time, the Baltic country was hit by a series of massive DDoS attacks that lasted several days and partially paralyzed the country. The attacks targeted government institutions, banks and media outlets and resulted in a nationwide outage of online services. The incident, which was attributed to Russia, marked one of the first large-scale cyberattacks on a sovereign state and highlighted the potential dangers posed by military cyber operations.

The 2014 attack on Sony Pictures, which was attributed to North Korea, also shows the scope and consequences of cyber warfare. In this case, the attack targeted a private company to prevent the release of a film critical of the North Korean government. The attack resulted in significant damage to the company's IT systems, the release of sensitive data, and significant economic damage. Although this attack did not hit a military target in the traditional sense, it shows how cyber warfare can also be used to achieve political goals and exert economic pressure.

Military actors also use techniques such as phishing and social engineering to exploit people's vulnerabilities. Phishing attacks, which use fake emails or messages to trick users into revealing confidential information or installing malicious software, are a common method of gaining access to sensitive data. Social engineering goes a step further and attempts to directly manipulate people to gain access to systems or information. These techniques are particularly dangerous because they are often difficult to detect and can bypass traditional security measures.

In modern cyber warfare, military systems and infrastructures are increasingly interconnected, making them simultaneously more efficient but also more vulnerable to attack. One example of this is the increasing reliance on satellite networks to monitor, communicate and control military operations. These satellite systems are often a target of cyberattacks because they play a central role in coordinating forces. A successful attack on a military satellite system could disrupt communications networks, affect troop movements and interrupt the flow of information between different command posts.

However, the use of cyber weapons is not only used by major powers such as the US, Russia and China. Smaller nations, terrorist organisations and private hacker groups are also increasingly turning

POSSIBILITIES OF CYBERWARS

to cyber technologies to achieve their political and military goals. This makes cyber warfare a global phenomenon that is not limited to conflicts between states. Actors such as the Islamic State or other terrorist groups have shown that they are capable of carrying out cyber attacks to hit both military and civilian targets.

The question of attribution, i.e. the precise identification of attackers, is one of the greatest challenges in cyber warfare. Since cyber attacks are often carried out via obfuscated networks, anonymization services and proxy servers, it is often difficult for victim states to determine exactly who is responsible for an attack. This leads to considerable diplomatic tensions and complicates international cooperation in combating cyber warfare.

Overall, it is clear that the technological mechanisms of cyber warfare are extremely complex and diverse. The ongoing development of new attack and defense techniques poses enormous challenges for both military actors and civilian infrastructures. As technology continues to develop rapidly, the threat of military cyber attacks will also continue to increase in the coming years, requiring constant adaptation of defense strategies.

A central element of modern military cyber warfare is the role of **automated attack and defense systems**, particularly through the use of **artificial intelligence (AI)** and **machine learning** (ML). These technologies enable cyber operations to scale complex attacks in ways that cannot be achieved by traditional methods. For example, by using AI, attackers can identify and exploit vulnerabilities in networks in real time without relying on human intervention. This results in the speed and precision of cyber attacks increasing dramatically.

In the area of **defensive strategies,** AI and ML have also taken on an important role. Many modern **intrusion detection systems (IDS)** use machine learning to detect anomalies in network traffic and thus ward off potential attacks. This means that systems continuously process new data and learn to identify the increasingly sophisticated attacks.

Behavioral detection becomes a key mechanism here, as abnormal user activity can immediately raise alarms and ward off potential threats.

threat of zero-day exploits remains one of the biggest challenges. Since these vulnerabilities are by definition still unknown and no countermeasures have been developed, even the most advanced defense systems are vulnerable. Governments therefore invest considerable resources in detecting and protecting against such attacks. There is also a lucrative black market for zero-day exploits, where such vulnerabilities are sold to the highest bidder - often to governments or private actors who use this information to launch targeted cyberattacks.

Attacks on critical infrastructure , particularly those known as "smart grids," are a growing threat. As power grids, water supplies, and transportation systems become digitized and interconnected, they become attractive targets for attackers. An attack on a smart grid, for example, could trigger widespread power outages that paralyze a country's civilian and military infrastructure. These attacks are particularly dangerous because they can often trigger a chain reaction in which a small attack can have devastating effects on the entire network.

Another central element of military cyber warfare is the use of **botnets,** which consist of thousands or even millions of compromised devices that can be used for coordinated attacks. These botnets can be used for **Distributed Denial of Service (DDoS)** attacks, in which servers and networks are overloaded with a flood of requests to make them inaccessible. Such attacks can be used especially in military conflicts to paralyze the enemy's communications or control systems, resulting in significant tactical disadvantages.

Unlike conventional attacks, where the weapons are clearly identifiable, **cyber weapons are often difficult to detect and attribute.** This invisibility complicates a state's ability to track attacks and respond appropriately. **Attribution** - identifying the originator of an attack - remains one of the biggest challenges in military cyber warfare. Attackers can cover their tracks by using proxies, **encrypted communication** channels and **TOR networks**, making them extremely difficult to clearly identify. This leads to an increased risk of misinterpretation, misunderstanding and possibly unprovoked counterattacks.

In addition to the technical aspects, military cyber warfare is increasingly being complemented by **psychological warfare**. Through the targeted use of **disinformation** and **propaganda** on social media, cyber warriors can manipulate public opinion and incite panic or uncertainty. This is particularly relevant in times of military conflict, where public support or trust in the government can be crucial. Attacking the credibility of news sources or spreading fake information can undermine public trust and thus cause political instability.

Also of note is the **rise of "hacktivism"** - the use of hacking methods by activists to achieve political or social goals. While states and large organizations are the main players in military cyberwarfare, **non-state actors** such as hacker groups have also taken on an important role. Groups such as **Anonymous** or **LulzSec** have shown that even small, well-organized units are capable of carrying out devastating attacks. While some of these groups claim to act in the name of "justice," their actions can often have unpredictable consequences because they operate unregulated and without government control.

In conclusion, **military cyber warfare is constantly evolving**. As technology advances at an ever-increasing pace, new threats will emerge that cannot be foreseen today. **Quantum computing,** for example, has the potential to radically change the way encryption and security measures work. Once this technology matures, many of the current security protocols used in cyber warfare could become obsolete. States and military actors will be forced to constantly adapt their strategies and develop new defense methods to keep up with the changing threats.

Impact on national infrastructure and critical systems

Attacks in military cyber warfare often focus on the vulnerability of national infrastructures, particularly critical systems that are essential to maintaining daily life. These infrastructures, including power grids, water distribution, transportation systems, and communications networks, are increasingly digitized and thus more vulnerable to cyberattacks. Attacks on these vital infrastructures can have catastrophic effects on the affected population, as they not only hit military targets but also significantly disrupt civilian life.

A prominent example of the vulnerability of critical infrastructure is the attack on the Ukrainian power grid in 2015. Russian hackers penetrated Ukraine's power grid and left hundreds of thousands of people without electricity for hours. This attack clearly demonstrated how military cyber warfare can directly target the population and massively disrupt civilian life. The attack on Ukraine affected not only households, but also hospitals, transport systems and communication networks, highlighting an escalation in the threat of cyber warfare.

Along with power grids, **water supply systems are** among the most critical infrastructures at risk of cyberattacks. A successful attack on waterworks or pumping stations could disrupt or contaminate the water supply of entire cities. This threat is particularly dangerous because water is essential for daily survival and public health. In a military context, the targeted disruption of water supplies could significantly weaken the moral and physical resilience of the population.

Transport systems are also increasingly the target of cyberattacks, especially in countries that rely heavily on digital technologies to manage traffic flows. From taking over traffic control systems to manipulating air or rail networks, attackers could massively disrupt the transport of goods and people. In the event of a cyberwar, this could lead to logistical problems that seriously affect supply chains for food, medical equipment and military resources. Disrupting such systems could not only cause economic damage, but also trigger panic and chaos among the affected population.

The vulnerabilities of national **communications systems** are also a critical threat in cyber warfare. Attacks on cellular networks, the internet, or satellite systems could disrupt communications between government, military, and civilians. The impact of such attacks is severe: without reliable means of communication, coordinated defense, emergency response, and proper administration cannot take place. Especially in emergency situations, continuous communication is essential to save lives and maintain control of the situation. One example was the attack on the Viasat satellite communications network in 2022, where a cyberattack related to the Russian-Ukrainian conflict knocked out internet services across Ukraine, affecting the country's ability to coordinate its defense.

Another often overlooked but equally critical target of cyberattacks are **hospitals and medical facilities.** These are increasingly digitized to improve patient care, but this digitization has also made them more vulnerable to cyber warriors. Cyberattacks affecting medical devices or patient data could have life-threatening consequences, especially when attackers target hospitals' life-saving systems. In 2020, for example, a hospital in Düsseldorf was hit by a ransomware attack, resulting in patients having to be transferred to other hospitals because the hospital's IT systems were down. This shows that cyberwarfare not only causes economic or military damage, but can also have direct consequences for human life.

Financial systems are also frequently targeted by cyberattacks, as they play a central role in a country's economic stability. A successful cyber operation that disrupts a country's banking system could cause severe economic disruption, trigger panic in financial markets, and undermine public confidence in the stability of the economy. A coordinated attack on banks, for example, could prevent salaries from being paid, restrict access to cash, and make credit card payments impossible. This would have far-reaching effects on the ability of businesses to operate and on the daily lives of citizens, who might be unable to purchase basic goods and services.

In addition to the direct impact on critical infrastructure, cyberattacks also have profound **economic consequences.** The loss of data, disruption of production chains and destruction of digital assets can cost companies and states millions, if not billions. During a military conflict, these economic damages can severely affect a state's ability to finance its defense and provide for its population. Cyberwarfare aims not only at immediate physical destruction, but also at undermining a country's economic backing by destroying the foundations of its digital economy.

The long-term **consequences of cyberattacks on national infrastructure** not only affect the immediate outages, but also the public's confidence in the stability of their society. In an increasingly interconnected world where almost all areas of life depend on digital technology, a successful cyberattack can undermine trust in the state and its ability to provide basic services. This can lead to social unrest, panic and general insecurity, which further weakens state authority.

restoring damaged systems is often a lengthy and expensive process. While some systems can be restored quickly after an attack, more complex infrastructure such as power grids or communications systems require weeks or months to fully return to operation. These delays could have devastating consequences during a military conflict, especially if the adversary is able to launch repeated cyberattacks and thus undermine recovery efforts.

Overall, it is clear that cyber warfare can affect a country's national infrastructure in a variety of ways. From energy and water supplies to transportation systems to healthcare and communications networks, all of these systems are potential targets whose destruction or disruption can have devastating effects on the daily lives and safety of the affected population. The more a country depends on digital systems, the more vulnerable it is to the potentially catastrophic consequences of cyberattacks. This form of warfare shifts the front lines from physical battlefields to the digital networks that keep modern society running.

Cyberwar and Disinformation: Manipulation of Public Opinion

Another key aspect of military cyber warfare is the targeted spread of **disinformation**. This does not only involve direct cyber attacks on infrastructure, but also influencing and manipulating public opinion. This type of warfare, also known as **information warfare**, is increasingly used by states and non-state actors to weaken the psychological resilience of populations, influence political decisions and undermine trust in institutions.

Disinformation in cyber warfare is often spread through digital channels such as **social media, news portals** and **fake news websites**. Hacker groups and state-sponsored cyber agencies use these platforms to deliberately spread false information and create chaos or confusion. The high prevalence of social media means that fake news can reach millions of people in a matter of seconds, making it extremely difficult to distinguish truth from fiction. This often happens so subtly that the population does not even notice how their perception is being manipulated.

A well-known example of a large-scale disinformation campaign in the context of cyber warfare is Russia's influence on the **2016 US presidential election.** Russian cyber groups used a mix of **hacking** and **disinformation operations** to destabilize the political climate in the US. By hacking email accounts of high-ranking politicians and spreading fake news on social networks, the actors tried to sow distrust in the democratic process and influence public opinion. These types of attacks show that military cyber warfare goes far beyond conventional methods and that manipulating political discourse has become a central strategy.

Another example is the large-scale Russian disinformation campaign during the **annexation of Crimea** in 2014. In addition to the physical invasion of Crimea, Russia relied on a massive media offensive to confuse and polarize the population both locally and internationally. Through targeted false reports and the use of bots and trolls on social networks, the Russian authorities managed to obscure the true course of events and change the public perception of the events in their favor.

Such tactics are based on creating **uncertainty and confusion.** By simultaneously spreading contradictory information, the public is brought into a state where it is difficult to distinguish fact from fiction. This undermines trust in media reporting and in the institutions responsible for disseminating reliable information. As a result, this can lead to a division in society as different groups begin to believe alternative narratives, often driven by political or ideological interests.

The **use of "deepfakes"** - fake videos or audio recordings created using artificial intelligence - is a particularly dangerous development in disinformation campaigns. Deepfakes can enable attackers to generate and spread convincing but fake statements from political leaders or other influential people. This technology makes it even more difficult to verify the authenticity of information and could play a central role in cyberwarfare in the future by undermining the credibility of decision-makers or deliberately fueling conflict.

In addition to directly spreading false information, cyber warriors also aim to **intensify existing social and political tensions.** By using **algorithm manipulation** in social networks and promoting extremist or polarizing content, cyber warfare can exacerbate existing social conflicts. This is often done by deliberately spreading content that triggers emotions such as fear, anger or mistrust. One example of this is influencing debates on sensitive topics such as migration, racism or religious tensions. Such attacks aim to destabilize the social fabric of a country and turn people against each other, while the actual attackers remain in the background.

In many cases, disinformation campaigns aim to **undermine trust in democratic institutions.** By spreading false information about elections, corruption or the justice system, attackers can question the legitimacy of the state order. This has been a recurring pattern, especially during elections in Western democracies, where actors have sought to undermine the population's trust in the democratic process. By sowing doubts about the independence of the judiciary or the transparency of electoral processes, cyberwarfare actors can weaken a country's political stability.

A particularly perfidious strategy in military cyber warfare is to deliberately spread **false information in crisis situations** . During natural disasters, pandemics or military conflicts, attackers can spread false news about emergency response, relief services or the state of infrastructure. This tactic aims to create panic and undermine the ability of government or relief organizations to respond effectively to the crisis. In 2020, during the COVID-19 pandemic, numerous false reports circulated around the world, spreading uncertainty about the effectiveness of vaccines or the availability of medical supplies. Such cyber campaigns pose a serious threat to public health and safety.

Propaganda and **disinformation** are not new, but digitalization has given these tactics a new dimension in military cyber warfare. While traditional propaganda campaigns often relied on physical means such as posters, radio or television broadcasts, modern cyber warriors can operate much faster and more precisely through the internet and social media. In addition, the digital world allows disinformation to reach large parts of the population without the source of the information being clearly identifiable. This makes it difficult for governments and defenders to respond quickly and effectively to such threats.

Psychological warfare in the digital space aims to weaken the morale of the population and create confusion. By deliberately spreading fear and doubt about the government's ability to ensure national security, cyber warriors can put the population into a state of uncertainty. This strategy is particularly effective when combined with physical cyberattacks on infrastructure, leading to an escalation of uncertainty and panic. When people can no longer rely on their news sources, their government or their infrastructure, it can significantly weaken a nation's resilience.

To counter the threats posed by disinformation campaigns in military cyber warfare, states must develop comprehensive

counterstrategies . This requires closer cooperation between governments, technology companies and the media to identify and debunk disinformation more quickly. **Media literacy initiatives** play a central role in this, as they help the population to recognize fake news and be more critical of the information they consume. Likewise, the development of technologies to detect deepfakes and other manipulative content is an essential part of defending against such threats.

Overall, it is clear that manipulating public opinion is a powerful tool in military cyber warfare. By spreading disinformation and propaganda, attackers can cause far-reaching social and political consequences without firing a single shot. This form of warfare aims to undermine trust in institutions, exacerbate societal tensions, and weaken the resilience of nations from within.

Dangers to the Civilian Population: Legal, Social and Health Consequences

The dangers that military cyberwarfare poses to civilian populations are diverse and far-reaching. Cyberattacks that specifically target civilian infrastructure can have devastating effects, both in the short and long term. **From human rights violations** to **social inequalities** and **health threats,** military cyberwarfare poses a serious threat to the security and well-being of affected populations.

A key problem is the **blurring of the boundaries between civilian and military targets.** In traditional wars, military targets were usually clearly separated from civilian areas. In cyber warfare, however, these spheres often overlap. Civilian infrastructures - such as hospitals, energy supplies, transport systems and water supplies - are often so closely linked to military networks that attacks on these systems affect both the civilian population and military facilities. This means that the civilian population becomes an unwanted target and is drawn directly into the conflict.

Attacks on healthcare systems are a particularly worrying aspect of cyber warfare. As mentioned above, the increasing use of digital technologies in healthcare has improved the efficiency of patient care, but at the same time has increased vulnerability to cyberattacks. Cyber warriors could, for example, **hack medical databases,** tamper with medical equipment, or paralyze hospital operations through **ransomware attacks** . The consequences of such attacks are not only financial - they directly endanger human lives. When life-saving equipment such as ventilators, heart monitors, or drug dosing systems are disabled, people who are in no way involved in military conflict can die.

The **psychological impact on civilians** is also immense. In a scenario where basic services such as electricity, water and communications are disrupted by cyberattacks, fear and insecurity among the population can increase dramatically. Especially in areas already affected by military conflict, such attacks can further exacerbate an already tense situation. People who live in constant uncertainty are more likely to develop **stress symptoms, anxiety** or **post-traumatic stress disorder (PTSD).** The psychological consequences of a cyberwar can therefore have an impact on the collective well-being of an entire society far beyond the actual attacks.

In addition to the physical and psychological threat, civilians also face **social and legal challenges** . In the context of cyberwar, the **digital divide** – that is, unequal access to technology and digital resources – can further exacerbate existing social inequalities. Populations with no or limited access to modern technologies are often less able to defend themselves or recover from the effects of a cyberattack. For example, a wealthy urban area may have the resources to respond quickly to an attack on the power grid, while poorer or rural areas may be left without power for days, causing even greater suffering for the people living there.

On a legal level, cyberwar poses a major challenge to existing international laws. While **international humanitarian law** , particularly the Geneva Conventions, aims to protect civilians in war, it is unclear how these laws can be applied to cyberwar. **Cyberattacks on civilian**

infrastructure could be considered a violation of international law, especially if they directly target civilians. However, the question of **accountability** is complicated because in cyberspace it is often difficult to accurately identify and hold attackers accountable. States can use proxy actors or private hacker groups to carry out attacks without having to officially take responsibility.

Another legal issue in military cyberwarfare concerns the **privacy and data rights** of civilians. Cyberattacks can lead to the theft of sensitive personal data, including medical, financial and legal information. In many cases, the individuals affected are not even aware that their data has been compromised, which further increases the long-term consequences of such attacks. When state actors conduct cyberattacks on civilian targets, they could exploit the personal data of the affected population to establish surveillance systems or suppress political opposition.

Social **inequality** is also exacerbated by **digital infrastructure** itself. In regions where digital transformation is already well advanced, a cyberattack could have devastating consequences for the economy and daily life, while less developed regions may be more resilient to digital attacks because they are less dependent on interconnected systems. However, this creates a double risk: while highly developed regions are more vulnerable due to their dependence on technology, less developed regions do not have the resources to defend themselves effectively or recover quickly after an attack.

Long-term **health consequences** of cyber warfare should not be underestimated either. Attacks on **public health systems** or the targeted destruction of **medical care networks** could have catastrophic effects in crisis situations such as pandemics or natural disasters. If cyber attacks paralyze a country's medical infrastructure during a crisis, they can lead to an unnecessarily high number of deaths caused by the lack of medical care. Cyber attacks on health systems could worsen the effects of epidemics, hinder health care in war zones and, in the long term, undermine the population's trust in their health infrastructure.

Education is also an area that can be severely affected by cyberattacks. In an increasingly digitalized world, educational institutions rely on digital platforms, networks and online learning resources. Cyberattacks on educational institutions can not only disrupt classes, but also put sensitive data of students and teachers at risk. Such attacks could have a long-term impact on the educational level and future prospects of the generations affected. Especially in regions that are already suffering from conflict or economic crises, the failure of educational institutions due to cyberattacks could set back an entire generation.

An often overlooked but equally important aspect is the **ethical questions** that arise in relation to cyber warfare. As civilian populations become increasingly involved in military cyber conflicts, a **moral dilemma arises** as to how far states may go in implementing their cyber warfare strategies. Should there be ethical limits prohibiting the use of cyber attacks against civilian targets, even when those targets indirectly support military functions? Distinguishing **between legitimate military targets and civilian casualties** is becoming increasingly difficult in cyberspace, necessitating an urgent debate on the ethical and legal frameworks of cyber warfare.

The growing reliance on **Internet of Things (IoT)** devices and connected systems also poses an increasing threat. More and more everyday objects – from household appliances to vehicles – are connected to the internet and can potentially be hacked. An attack on IoT systems could have far-reaching consequences, from control of transport systems to physical damage to connected devices. So civilians are in many ways defenseless against the effects of cyberwar, as their everyday technologies can become weapons in a digital conflict.

In summary, military cyber warfare poses significant and diverse risks to the civilian population. From direct physical impacts from attacks on critical infrastructure to long-term psychological, social and legal consequences: the civilian population is often the unwilling victim in a cyber war. International agreements, ethical debates and new defense strategies must be urgently developed to ensure the protection of civilians in the digital age.

Future Scenarios: The Rise of Autonomous Cyber Weapons and the Intensification of Conflicts

As technology advances, new dimensions in military cyber warfare are opening up that could radically change the way conflicts are fought in the future. One of the most dangerous developments is the **rise of autonomous cyber weapons**, capable of conducting attacks, making decisions, and dynamically adapting to their environment without human intervention. This development poses not only technological risks, but also moral and political challenges that could have far-reaching consequences for the global security architecture.

Autonomous cyber weapons are an extension of the **concept of autonomous weapons systems,** such as armed drones or robots, already used in military operations today. These systems, which are able to identify and attack targets without the immediate intervention of a human operator, have the potential to increase the efficiency and speed of military operations. In cyberspace, this could mean that autonomous programs would be able to detect and exploit vulnerabilities in enemy networks in real time, while adapting and defending their own attacks.

One of the main concerns regarding these systems is the risk that they could **get out of control**. Autonomous cyber weapons based on machine learning could make decisions that were not intended by their developers. These systems could lead to unforeseen escalations, for example by carrying out attacks on civilian infrastructure without distinguishing between military and civilian targets. Another risk is that such systems could be hacked or taken over by other actors, which would make it extremely difficult to clearly assign responsibility for an attack.

The development of **artificial intelligence (AI)-enabled cyberweapons** also offers the potential for use in broader **cyber cold wars** . Similar to the nuclear arms race of the 20th century, states could enter into a technological race to develop the most powerful and effective cyberweapons. This could lead to an increasing militarization of cyberspace, with states seeking to automate their defense systems and continually develop new offensive capabilities. The danger here is that such an arms race could be subject to **miscalculations** and **unintended attacks** that could quickly escalate into open conflict.

Another worrying scenario is the possibility of **cyber weapons that can replicate themselves** . Such weapons could use mechanisms similar to computer worms to spread through enemy networks, modifying themselves in the process to make them more difficult to detect and defend against. This type of "smart cyber weapon" could allow attackers to launch an attack with minimal effort, while the weapon itself maximizes its reach and impact. Such a scenario poses the risk that a single attack could trigger an uncontrollable **chain reaction** that could quickly spread globally.

These risks raise the pressing question of how to ensure **accountability and control** in such an environment. In traditional law of war, there are clear rules on how to conduct war, including the distinction between military and civilian targets and the responsibility of commanders for the actions of their troops. However, in cyberwar, especially in the context of autonomous systems, it becomes increasingly difficult to assign such responsibilities. If an autonomous cyberweapon hits a civilian target or carries out a devastating attack, who is to blame - the developer of the system, the state deploying it, or the system itself? This **ethical gray area** will become one of the greatest challenges of the future.

In addition to the technological risks, there are also questions about the **social and political consequences** of the increasing automation of cyber warfare. States may be increasingly tempted to rely on autonomous systems because they cause fewer human casualties and can deliver quick, effective results. However, this could lower the barrier to using cyber attacks and lead to an **increase in smaller, faster conflicts** that may not end in open war but can still cause significant damage. The idea that a state could respond to a cyber attack within minutes without having to rely on diplomatic or military escalation mechanisms could further destabilize the global security situation.

Another future scenario related to advancing technology is the possibility of a **global cyberwar** that would affect all aspects of modern life. In such a scenario, not only military and government networks could be attacked, but also all **civilian infrastructures** that rely on digital technologies. This would lead to widespread disruption of energy supplies, transport, healthcare and the economy. The **dependence on digital systems** makes modern societies extremely vulnerable to such attacks, and the possibility of multiple states or actors launching massive cyberattacks simultaneously could plunge the world into an unprecedented crisis.

Such a scenario could also lead to **non-state actors** playing a larger role. In a global cyberwar, terrorist organizations, criminal groups and even individuals could be able to carry out devastating attacks that would normally only be available to states. The decentralization of cyberwarfare means that it will become increasingly difficult to maintain control of the conflict as there are more and more actors capable of engaging in the attacks.

On the other hand, advancing technology also offers opportunities for **preventive measures and security mechanisms** to mitigate such threats. States and international organizations are working to develop **cyber defense systems** that are able to detect and repel attacks in real time. This includes both strengthening **cyber resilience** - the ability to recover quickly from an attack - and developing technologies for **early threat detection**. Machine learning and AI can help to identify patterns in networks that indicate impending attacks and take appropriate countermeasures.

In addition, there are initiatives for **international cooperation** in combating cyber warfare. The **Tallinn Rules** , an attempt to apply international law to cyberspace, represent a first step towards creating a legal framework for the use of cyber weapons. These rules aim to regulate the use of cyber attacks and clarify the responsibility of states. However, such agreements are often difficult to enforce because cyberspace is borderless and identifying attackers is extremely difficult in many cases.

A key approach to preventing future conflicts in cyberspace is to **strengthen international norms** and **confidence-building measures.** States could agree on certain basic principles, such as prohibiting attacks on civilian infrastructure or restricting the use of autonomous cyber weapons. Such agreements could help limit the arms race in cyberspace, similar to the non-proliferation of nuclear weapons. But even in such a scenario, the problem remains that many actors, including non-state actors, do not feel bound by international agreements.

In summary, the world is entering a new era of warfare in which **cyber warfare could be** increasingly dominated by **autonomous systems** and **AI-guided weapons** . The potential dangers these technologies pose range from unintended escalations to global crises affecting all aspects of modern life. The ability to manage such threats while ensuring that the use of cyber weapons remains ethically and legally justifiable will become one of the greatest challenges of the coming decades.

International Cooperation and Prevention of Cyberwar

Given the increasing threat of military cyberattacks, international cooperation is becoming a crucial element to prevent future cyberwars and ensure security in global cyberspace. The nature of cyberwar makes it particularly complex, as it knows no physical borders, international law is difficult to apply in many cases, and actors are often hard to identify. To address these challenges, states, international organizations, and private companies must work closely together to develop **global cyber norms, defense strategies**, and **legal frameworks**.

An important step towards stronger **international regulation** of cyber warfare was the **creation of the Tallinn Rules.** Originally developed in 2013 by a group of international legal experts under the auspices of NATO, these rules aim to apply international law to cyberspace. The Tallinn Rules clarify under which circumstances cyber attacks are considered acts of war and how **international humanitarian law** can be applied in the context of cyber warfare. They also address issues such as the attribution of attacks, state responsibility, and the distinction between civilian and military targets.

However, the Tallinn Rules are **not binding** and are not fully recognized by some states. A major problem remains the enforcement of such agreements, as cyberspace makes it difficult to monitor violations and hold states accountable. Despite these challenges, the Tallinn Rules are an important step in the right direction as they set the framework for future **international agreements on the use of cyber weapons. They help** to provide clarity on **states' responsibilities in cyberspace and provide a basis for diplomatic negotiations on cybersecurity issues.**

In addition to such legal frameworks, international **confidence and security measures also play** a crucial role in preventing cyber wars. **Confidence** -building measures (CBMs) are strategies that aim to reduce tensions between states and minimize the risk of misunderstandings or unintentional escalations in cyberspace. An example of such a measure is the **exchange of information about cyber attacks** or the establishment of communication channels between the cyber defense centers of different states in order to be able to respond more quickly in the event of an attack.

International organizations such as the **United Nations (UN)** and the **Organization for Security and Cooperation in Europe (OSCE)** have also begun to address cybersecurity more intensively. The **UN Group of Governmental Experts** (UN GGE) has published several reports proposing guidelines and norms for the responsible use of cyber weapons. A key aspect of this work is to develop **norms of behavior** that deter states from launching attacks on critical civilian infrastructure and restrict the use of cyberspace for acts of war.

NATO plays a leading role in coordinating the cyber defence of its member states. With the establishment of the **NATO Cooperative Cyber Defence Centre of Excellence (CCDCOE), the Alliance has created a platform to** share knowledge on cyber threats, develop common defence strategies and strengthen the cybersecurity capabilities of its members. NATO has also officially recognised cyber attacks as a potential **activation basis for** the Alliance's Article 5, which states that an attack on one member state is considered an attack on all. This underlines the growing importance of cyberspace in NATO's global security strategy.

In addition to government efforts, there is also increasing collaboration between **governments and the private sector.** With much of the critical infrastructure in the hands of private companies, it is crucial that these companies are involved in defending against cyberattacks. Companies such as Microsoft, Google and Cisco play a key role in cybersecurity as they develop technologies used by both governments and private individuals. Increased **public-private partnership** is therefore essential to improve cyber defense capabilities and ensure that both government and private actors can respond effectively to threats in cyberspace.

One example of such collaboration is the **Cybersecurity Tech Accord,** a global coalition of over 150 technology companies committed to working together to improve cybersecurity. These companies are committing to, among other things, preventing cyberattacks, better protecting their customers, and not developing products or services that could be used for malicious purposes. Initiatives like this show that solving the threat of cyberwarfare is not in the hands of governments alone, but that the private sector must also play a central role.

In addition to cooperation at the technical and legal levels, states also need to continue to develop their **cyber defense capabilities** . This includes not only strengthening **technological capabilities** to detect and defend against cyberattacks, but also training and upskilling cybersecurity **professionals** . Many countries face an acute shortage of qualified cybersecurity experts, which significantly limits the ability of states to defend themselves against increasingly complex attacks. To address this problem, some states have launched programs to develop young talent in cybersecurity and strengthen cooperation between universities, the military and the private sector.

Another important aspect of cyberwar prevention is the development of **early detection systems** and **early warning networks** that can identify potential threats before they occur. Technologies such as **artificial intelligence (AI) and big data analytics** can help monitor **suspicious activity** on the internet, identify vulnerabilities in networks, and prevent potential attacks before they are realized. However, these systems are only as effective as the data they process and the ability of states to respond quickly to warning signals.

Despite these efforts, a major problem remains unsolved: the **attribution of cyberattacks.** Because cyberattacks are often disguised and carried out through multiple servers in different countries, it is difficult to clearly identify the originator of an attack. This problem makes it difficult to hold states or groups accountable and to take effective countermeasures. Although there is progress in developing technologies to track cyberattacks, attribution remains one of the biggest challenges in the fight against cyberwarfare.

In conclusion, **international cooperation** and **prevention of cyberwar** should help ensure security in global cyberspace in the coming years. (??) Given the constantly evolving technologies and the increasing sophistication of cyberattacks, states and organizations must continuously adapt their strategies and develop new mechanisms for cooperation. Only through comprehensive cooperation, both at the state and private level, can we effectively contain the threat of cyberwarfare and create a safer digital future.

*

Conclusions:

The analysis of cyberwar shows that this area of modern warfare is far more than just a technical phenomenon. Cyberwars affect all aspects of state and social life and have the potential to permanently change the future of the global security architecture. From the threat of targeted attacks on critical infrastructure to the increasing importance of industrial espionage and the psychological manipulation of individuals and societies - the effects of cyberwars are profound and complex.

The **dependence on digital technologies** in almost all areas of life means that states and societies are becoming increasingly vulnerable to cyberattacks. Critical infrastructures such as the power grid, water supply, transport and healthcare have become a prime target for cyber warriors. Attacks on these systems can not only cause economic damage but also endanger the lives of millions of people. The complexity of modern digital infrastructures makes it difficult to defend effectively against such attacks and requires extensive and long-term investments in cybersecurity.

In addition, the **lines between civilian and military targets** in cyber warfare are increasingly blurred. Many of the digital systems that are essential to civilian life also play a crucial role in military operations. This duality makes it difficult to define clear rules for the use of cyber weapons and minimize the risk of civilian casualties. The lack of international consensus on the legal status of cyber attacks and the rules of cyber conflict further exacerbates this problem.

The **role of states** as major actors in cyber warfare is underscored by the fact that many nations are investing significant resources in building **cyber warfare units** . These units are specialized in conducting both offensive and defensive operations in the digital space, drawing on sophisticated technologies and specialized professionals. Countries such as the United States, Russia and China have significantly expanded their cyber capabilities and are increasingly using cyber weapons as a central tool in their geopolitical strategies.

But states are not the only actors in cyber warfare. **Non-state groups** such as hacktivists, cybercriminals and private security companies also play an important role. While some of these groups are financially motivated, others pursue political or ideological goals that often conflict with state interests. The ability of these groups to act independently of state control and cause significant damage makes cyber warfare a particularly difficult area of modern conflict to control.

A crucial aspect of cyber warfare is also the **psychological component.** The targeted manipulation of fear, uncertainty and mistrust can be just as destructive as a physical attack. Attackers use disinformation campaigns and social engineering to undermine trust in state institutions, democratic processes and even in technology itself. This type of psychological warfare has the potential to destabilize society in the long term and exacerbate social tensions.

The future of cyber warfare will be heavily shaped by **technological developments** . **Advances in quantum computing,** artificial **intelligence** , and **autonomous weapons systems** have the potential to take cyber warfare to a new level. While quantum computers could crack existing encryption systems, AI-powered systems could carry out cyberattacks autonomously and in real time. Such developments will make defending against cyberattacks much more difficult and require new approaches to cybersecurity.

Despite these challenges, there is also the possibility of preventing the escalation of cyber conflicts through **international cooperation** . **The creation of binding international norms and rules** for the use of cyber weapons is essential to avoid uncontrolled cyber wars. This also includes the creation of mechanisms for **attribution** of cyber attacks in order to hold those responsible to account and prevent misjudgments.

In addition, it will be crucial that states and companies work more closely together to build **resilience against cyberattacks** . Companies play a central role in cyberwarfare, as they are often at the center of attacks that have both economic and security implications. Cooperation between public and private actors must be intensified to ensure the protection of critical infrastructure and restore trust in digital technologies.

Ultimately, it is clear that **digital space** is increasingly becoming the battlefield of the future. Cyberwars pose a serious threat to global security, and the international community must take urgent action to regulate and protect cyberspace. Without clear rules and effective defense strategies, the world could enter an era of uncontrolled digital conflict, the consequences of which could be unpredictable and devastating. It is time for states, companies and international organizations to work together to make cyberspace a safer place and keep the peace in the digital age.

This concludes this reflection on the **possibilities of cyberwar** and its future course. The various sections have shown that cyberwar is a complex and growing challenge, shaped by technological, legal, psychological and geopolitical factors. The future of cyberwar requires not only technological innovations, but also new approaches to international cooperation and cybersecurity to ensure peace and stability in the digital world.

*

Information sources:

Since this article is content-based and based on known information, it is a reproduction of current knowledge about cyber warfare from publicly available and established information sources.

Here are some example sources and subject areas that can serve as a reference for further study or detailed information:

1. Books and academic papers on cyber warfare:

  ○ Rid, Thomas: Cyber War Will Not Take Place. Oxford University Press, 2013.

  ○ Singer, PW, and Friedman, Allan: Cybersecurity and Cyberwar: What Everyone Needs to Know. Oxford University Press, 2014.

  ○ Clarke, Richard A., and Knake, Robert K.: Cyber War: The Next Threat to National Security and What to Do About It. Ecco, 2010.Clarke, Richard A., and Knake, Robert K.: Cyber War: The Next Threat to National Security and What to Do About It. Ecco, 2010.

2. Official reports and documents:

  ○ Reports from governments and organizations such as the European Union (e.g. NIS Directive) or the Cybersecurity and Infrastructure Security Agency (CISA) in the USA.

  ○ UN reports on international efforts and cyber diplomacy (e.g. work of the Open-ended Working Group (OEWG) on cybersecurity).

3. Media reports on significant cyber attacks:

  ○ The "Stuxnet" case: Reporting on the attack on the Iranian nuclear program.

  ○ Russian influence in the 2016 US elections: Various reports and analyses from The New York Times, The Guardian or BBC.

  ○ NotPetya and WannaCry attacks: Numerous articles, e.g. from Wired or The Verge.

4. Scientific articles and publications on quantum computing and artificial intelligence:

◦ Nature, Science and other academic journals provide deep insights into technological developments that could impact future cyberwar.

◦ Reports and articles on advances in quantum cryptography in computer science and information security journals.

5. Private cybersecurity companies and their reports:

◦ FireEye and CrowdStrike publish regular reports on threat analysis and the latest trends in cybersecurity.

◦ The Verizon Data Breach Investigations Report (DBIR) is an important annual source of information about cyberattacks.

6. International organizations and cooperations:

◦ Reports and publications of the NATO Cooperative Cyber Defence Centre of Excellence (CCDCOE).

◦ European Network and Information Security Agency (ENISA): Publications on strengthening cybersecurity capacities in the EU.

About this book:

The term "**cyberwar**" describes military or (even state-sponsored) conflicts that are fought through the use of technology in digital space. In contrast to traditional wars, in which physical weapons and soldiers are used on the battlefield, cyberwars shift to networks, computers and digital infrastructures. They aim to disrupt, manipulate or destroy communication systems, economic systems, government agencies and other critical infrastructures.

This book provides an overview of what makes cyberwar possible, what scenarios are conceivable and how such conflicts could develop in the future.

*

The author

Mr. Meier actually learned everything he knows from Mrs. Meier – and Mrs. Meier is actually a man.

If you want to know more, ask your trusted roofer, because doctors and pharmacists don't know anything about this either...

*

Also by 'Herr Meier'

Me hacker - you script kiddy !
Path to the Darknet
Surveillance mania
La folie de la surveillance... comment contourner ?
Hacken eines Computers
Hacking a computer
Hackear un computadora
Pirater un ordinateur
Hackear um computador
Möglichkeiten von Cyberkriegen
Possibilités de cyberguerres
Possibilities of cyberwars
Posibilidades de guerras cibernéticas
Possibilidades de guerra cibernética
Possibilità di guerre informatiche

Milton Keynes UK
Ingram Content Group UK Ltd.
UKHW020120221024
449869UK00010B/358